I JUST KEEP WONDERING

For further information, contact:
Tumblehome, Inc.
201 Newbury St, Suite 201
Boston, MA 02116
http://www.Thinc-science.org

Library of Congress Control Number 2019930021
ISBN 978-1-943431-44-1

Scheckel, Larry
I Just Keep Wondering / Larry Scheckel - 1st ed

Front cover science & technology icons: designed by Freepik from Flaticon
Front and back cover image credit: NASA/U. S. Geological Survey/Norman Kuring/Kathryn Hansen (modified)

Printed in Taiwan

10 9 8 7 6 5 4 3 2 1

I JUST KEEP WONDERING

121 Questions and Answers about Science and Other Stuff

Larry Scheckel

TUMBLEHOME, Inc.

Dedication

*This book is dedicated to my wife,
Ann Martin Scheckel.
For her love, companionship, devotion, support,
helpfulness, and suggestions. We have journeyed
through life together.*

Contents

Chapter One: The Exquisite Human Body

Chapter Two: All the Plants and Animals

Chapter Three: The Science of Food and Drink

Chapter Four: Remarkable People in Science

Chapter Five : The Science of the Heavens and Earth

Chapter Six: Art, Music, Sports, and Math

Chapter Seven: Incredible Technology

Chapter Eight: At the Fringes of Science

Chapter Nine: Science Mystery and History

Chapter Ten: Chemistry and the Atom

Chapter Eleven: How the World Works

Chapter Twelve: Stuff I Always Wondered About

Chapter One

The Exquisite Human Body

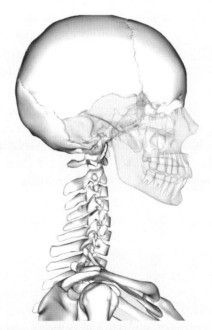

Wikimedia Commons :Rectus capitis anterior muscle

Larry Scheckel

Q1: Is too much sugar in your blood bad for you?

G lucose, a type of sugar that comes from carbohydrates found in food, is the main source of energy used by the body. Insulin, a hormone produced by the pancreas, helps the body's cells absorb glucose from our blood and use in our tissues.

When we eat, our blood glucose level rises. This increase signals the pancreas to release insulin so that the blood glucose levels do not get too high. Some people do not make enough insulin, and some people's tissues are resistant to insulin, especially if they are overweight. In either of these conditions, blood glucose levels get too high (hyperglycemia), and the person has diabetes. Over time, diabetes can damage the kidneys, blood vessels, eyes, and cardiovascular system.

Doctors and nurses do blood glucose tests to check for diabetes. The most common screening test is the eight-hour fasting blood sugar (FBS). A reading between 70 and 100 milligrams per deciliter (mg/dl) is good. Any reading above 100 may be reason for concern.

The other end of the spectrum is hypoglycemia, or not having enough sugar in the blood. The blood glucose reading will be low. Dangers from low blood glucose include seizures, unconsciousness, and brain damage. Hypoglycemia is rare except in diabetic people who have received too much insulin.

Many people avoid sugar for very good reasons. Eating too much sugar is a sure way to gain weight. Too much sugar can also rot your teeth. But there are several other good reasons to keep blood sugar levels in check.

High blood sugar ages the body in several ways. Diabetes leads to a shorter life span, speeds up the aging process, and makes the skin look older. High blood sugar levels seem to damage a protein that helps protect against Alzheimer's disease, so diabetes is also a risk factor for Alzheimer's. High blood sugar can also lead to a decrease of brain activity in the hippocampus area of the brain. The hippocampus is important in memory, so a decrease in brain activity can make Alzheimer's symptoms worse.

There are two kinds of diabetes. Type I diabetes is caused by damaged islet cells in the pancreas not putting out sufficient insulin. Type I diabetes is usually diagnosed in children and young adults, although it can appear at any age. Without insulin, these people's blood sugars can rise so high they can go into a diabetic coma. For this reason, people with type I diabetes must take insulin daily.

Type II diabetes, formerly known as adult-onset diabetes, runs in families, usually occurs later in life, and is usually associated with excessive weight gain. And that is where too much sugar comes in. Excessive sugar consumption (or excess consumption of calories in general) can cause the pounds to go on. Nowadays, we are seeing more and more type II diabetes even among young people. Patient with type II diabetes still make insulin, so they don't go into diabetic coma, but they may still suffer from the long-term effects of diabetes: heart disease, foot ulcers or amputations, kidney disease, or blindness.

So, in short, the answer is yes! Too much sugar in the blood is bad for you, and yes, eating too much sugar increases aging. Sometimes it seems that life is just not fair. Many people have asked themselves, how can something that tastes sooo good, like fudge, be sooo bad for you? Perhaps it comes down to moderation. One piece of fudge, OK. Two pieces, too much.

Q2: When you get your hair wet, why does it look darker?

When hair is dry, light striking it bounces off all its surfaces and between hair strands, which reflect a lot of different wavelengths of light. The hair looks lighter and brighter.

The same is true for glass. Glass is clear when it is a glass pane, but if broken into tiny particles, the glass becomes almost sand-like and looks white. It reflects a lot of light.

When they are wet, hair strands get closer together. Wet strands of hair adhere to one another better than dry strands. The water smooths the surfaces, and more light can penetrate deeper into the hair rather than being reflected. More light is absorbed, less light is reflected, hence darker-looking hair.

In addition, the light rays are subject to what is called total internal reflection inside the film of water around the hair strands. That means the light is trapped in the water by being reflected back in and not allowed to come out.

Human hair has some unusual uses. Strands of human hair provide a method to measure relative humidity, which is the amount of moisture in the air. Hair gets slightly longer when it is humid and shorter when the air is dryer. The hair hygrometer, which measures relative humidity, uses blond hair, with oils removed, under tension. The changing hair length is magnified by a series of levers and a needle gauge to obtain the reading. The first hair hygrometer was used in 1783.

Q3: Can aching joints predict the weather?

It is very difficult to prove a cause-and-effect relationship between weather and arthritis pain because there are so many variables. Those variables include temperature, humidity, barometric pressure, rainfall, sunshine, thunderstorm activity, purity of the air, and ionization of the air. Some studies show a link, while others are inconclusive. There are conflicting opinions and still no definitive agreement as to whether the weather has any effect on arthritis.

Some experiments indicate that 70 percent of people with arthritis are "weather sensitive." As bad weather approaches, they feel pain, soreness, and stiffness in their fingers, knees, hips, and shoulders. Many people feel that they can predict the onset of rain. We've all heard the expression "feeling under the weather."

Scientists do not believe that climatic or weather changes actually cause arthritis. But it seems likely that weather changes influence the amount of pain or discomfort felt by arthritis sufferers. Women seem to be more affected than men.

Temperature and humidity appear to be the biggest factors. Muscles, tendons, bones, and scar tissue have different densities, so cold and dampness expand and contract them in different ways. Warmth from a hot bath or heat packs can often help to ease pain by relaxing muscles. Ice packs, on the other hand, can decrease inflammation in the joints.

Barometric pressure also has an effect. In rheumatoid arthritis, joints are already inflamed and under pressure. If the barometric pressure drops, as when a low pressure comes through in advance of rainy weather, tissues can swell, causing more pain. In a 1961 study in Philadelphia, volunteers with arthritic conditions were placed in a climate-controlled windowless building. Many reported symptoms with a rise in humidity and decrease in temperature and barometric pressure.

Another factor is mood. People generally feel better when weather is warm, dry, and sunny. When foul weather sets in, people's moods may follow.

Q4: Why are boys' and girls' voices so different?

· ·

The short answer: Boys have longer vocal cords resulting in lower-pitched voices, while girls have shorter vocal cords that produce higher pitches.

When we talk or sing, air comes from the lungs and passes through the larynx, which is located in the throat. The vocal cords, which are like stretched rubber bands, vibrate and produce the sounds we hear. The larynx in kids is small, and the vocal cords are thin. That is why kids have higher-pitched voices than adults.

Changes take place as boys and girls mature. Girls' voices get just a bit deeper, toward the bass. But as boys reach puberty, their voices change considerably. The larynx grows larger, and the vocal cords become longer and thicker. During puberty, the vocal cords for boys grow about 0.125 inch (3.2 millimeters) more per year compared to girls. Boys' voices become deeper, meaning lower in pitch. The vocal cords of adult females are 0.6 inch (15 millimeters) long on average. For a male, the norm is 0.9 inch (22 millimeters).

The male voice ranges from about 85 to 180 hertz. The female voice range is from 165 to 255 hertz. Remember that hertz is a measure of frequency, or vibrations per second. Higher hertz means a higher-frequency sound and therefore a higher pitch.

Every voice is unique, influenced by other parts of the vocal tract, including the tongue, palate, lips, cheeks, and the shape of the chest and neck. It's not surprising, then, that we can identify a person from his or her voice, even when we cannot see the person. It is the same with singing voices. Most everyone can pick out Willie Nelson's nasal twang singing "Whiskey River," or Elvis Presley belting out "Hound Dog."

You may notice that a person's voice sounds different on the telephone compared to talking with him or her face-to-face. All voices contain a range of pitches combined. We understand speech from the higher pitches. The telephone company cuts out the lower frequencies to help us better hear what a person is saying. All frequencies below 400 hertz and above 3,400 hertz are filtered out. This practice improves intelligibility and at the same time limits the bandwidth so more conversations can be carried by the electronic equipment. The same filtering is used with astronauts. Their voices came back from the moon crystal clear because NASA uses the same filtering techniques as the phone company.

One notices this effect or technique when watching movies or television programs. The media creators deliberately shift away from the "telephone voice" to add realism to the programming.

The human voice runs into its share of problems. There are speech impediments, of course. And most people will experience short-term hoarseness caused by colds and flu. People who use their voices for a living, such as radio and television announcers, teachers, and singers, can succumb to swollen, soft spots on their vocal cords. Those spots can become callused and hard, resulting in nodules. Even more serious are polyps that may require surgical removal.

When I was a kid, we had a neighbor near our farm outside of Seneca, Wisconsin, in Crawford County who was "deaf and dumb"—he could not hear or speak. That was the insensitive term everyone used at the time and in that locale. The neighbor, who was born deaf, was a very successful farmer and certainly was not dumb in the thinking sense. But it was my first realization that if we couldn't hear, it would be difficult to learn to speak.

Q5: Why do we sweat on hot days?
. . . .

S weating is the body's method of cooling itself. Humans sweat to maintain a healthy, normal body temperature. Adults have between 3 and 4 million sweat glands, which secrete a water and salt solution. This solution sits on the surface of the skin until it evaporates away, causing the body to cool. Sweating acts as our body's radiator.

Evaporation, going from a liquid to a vapor state, is a cooling process. It takes 540 calories (half a kilocalorie, which is the "big" kind of calorie we measure in food) to turn a gram of water into a gram of vapor. That heat must come from somewhere. It comes from the person's body, thereby cooling the body just a little bit. Evaporation of sweat from the skin takes place faster if the air is hot and dry. It helps if there is a breeze. That's why you see people fanning themselves in hot, sticky weather.

People sweat mostly due to physical exertion, but embarrassment, anger, or stress can also get the sweat glands pumping. Excessive sweating is termed hyperhidrosis, and not being able to sweat is called anhidrosis. If a person does not sweat enough, the core temperature of the body can go too high. As a rule, men sweat more than women. My grandmother told me that women don't sweat. They perspire, gleam, or glow!

A body temperature above 104°F (40°C) can be dangerous. Fevers can cause these extremely high temperatures. In its attempt to fight off infection, the body is producing more heat than it can get rid of. Such high fevers are often broken by periods of sweating and cooling.

High body temperature can also occur in sunstroke, heat prostration, or hyperthermia. Overexertion, adverse drug reaction, or prolonged exposure to high heat and humidity can result in overheating of the body. The elderly are especially vulnerable. So are workers who wear protective clothing, such as firefighters, bomb squad personnel, and hazmat employees.

The astronauts who walked on the moon, a total of 12 Americans, had space suits fitted with 300 feet (90 meters) of small tubes that carried chilled water. The liquid-cooled garment removed excess heat as the water circulated around the astronaut's entire body.

On June 7, 1984, the Gillette Company brought out an advertising campaign for their line of Dry Idea antiperspirants. In the advertisements, famous personalities always mentioned three "nevers" for their profession. The third "never" was always, "Never let them see you sweat." Fashion designer Donna Karan, actress Lauren Hutton, and comedian Elayne Boosler each had a television advertisement for Dry Idea. But the viewer favorite was Dan Reeves, head coach of the Denver Broncos. His three "nevers" for a winning coach were: "Never let the press pick your starting quarterback. Never take a last-place team lightly. And really, no matter what the score, never let 'em see you sweat."

Q6: Why are anabolic steroids harmful?

Anabolic steroids are synthetic protein-building compounds that mimic the effects of testosterone and other male sex hormones. In fact, they are synthetic derivatives of naturally occurring male testosterone. They speed up muscle recovery following exercise or injury. They also build muscle tissue and bone strength.

Athletes use steroids to build muscle strength and bulk. Weight lifters, baseball players, football players, track and field athletes, and body-building contestants are prime users. Steroids work by helping the body retain dietary protein, which aids in developing muscles. That's the lure for athletes.

There is a downside. Anabolic steroids can damage the liver, heart, and adrenal glands. Anabolic steroids cause acne, premature balding, and hypertension. In men, they can lead to smaller testicles, impotence, infertility, and the development of breasts. Testimony in the perjury trial of baseball slugger Barry Bonds hinted at the "feminization" side effects of long-term steroid use.

Steroids are bad news for adolescents. Anabolic steroids close the growth plates in teen bones. Once they're closed, they never open again. Teens can develop problems with bone growth, leaving them shorter than they could or should be.

Women who use these drugs can develop masculine characteristics such as body and facial hair, male pattern balding, and deepening of the voice.

Anabolic steroids can also cause behavioral problems, especially severe mood swings. Abusers can cycle between bouts of depression and feelings of invincibility, irritability, paranoid jealousy, aggression, and rage.

Steroids are banned from most competitions because of the health dangers and because they give contestants who use them an unfair advantage over competitors. Several decades ago, some athletes used the oral form. Worrisome liver damage concerns cropped up. Recently, athletes that use steroids have opted for shorter-lasting, water-soluble injections.

Steroids were banned by Major League Baseball in 1991, but the league didn't institute testing until 2003. Much attention was drawn to steroid use by Jose Canseco's 2005 autobiography *Juiced*, in which the former slugger detailed widespread use and implicated the Bay Area Laboratory Co-Operative (BALCO) as a distributor.

Q7: What causes floaters in the eye?
. . . .

The big cavernous part of the eye is filled with a jelly-like fluid called the vitreous humor. The vitreous humor makes up about two thirds of the volume of the eye. Floaters are small speck-like particles of protein (collagen), pigment, or embryonic remnants left over from when the eye was formed. These flecks stay suspended in the vitreous humor.

Most people have these semitransparent floaters trapped in the eye but tend not to notice them. Eyes have a way of adjusting to imperfections and distractions. We may see floaters when they are in our line of sight. We are most likely to notice floaters when looking at a plain background, such as the sky, a whiteboard, a bare wall, or anything bright. They can take on the shape of dots, squiggly lines, strands of thread, or cobwebs.

Because floaters are suspended in the eye fluid, they move as the eye moves. They seem to dart away whenever a person tries to "see" them or focus in on them. If you are distracted by a floater, the easiest thing to do is to move your eye around by looking in different directions, which will cause the fluid to swirl a bit and allow the floater to move out of the way. Looking up and down is more effective than looking from side to side.

Most floaters are harmless, and most everyone will see them at some point. As a person gets older, the collagen fibers shrink, clump together to form shreds, and accumulate in the vitreous humor. People between the ages of 50 and 70 see floaters most often, especially people who are nearsighted or who have had cataract surgery or have diabetes. Most folks learn to live with and ignore floaters, which tend to diminish in number and prominence over months and years.

In rare cases, floaters can be a precursor to retinal damage. A significant increase in the number of floaters could be a warning sign. Floaters accompanied with sudden flashes of white light could be a signal of a retinal tear or detachment. Best to see an eye doctor pronto. If caught in time, retinal damage can often be repaired by laser treatment.

A very rare surgical operation can be performed if floaters are so dense and numerous that vision is severely affected. The procedure, called a vitrectomy, calls for the vitreous fluid and the floater debris to be drained and replaced with a saltwater solution. The procedure is risky, with a high chance of complications.

Q8: Why do people have different blood types?

B lood is made of red and white blood cells, platelets, and plasma, which is the liquid the cells flow through. Red blood cells carry specific identifiers on their surface. These identifiers are called antigens. The antigens help our body's immune system recognize its own red blood type. There are four main ABO blood type groupings: A, B, AB, and O. The type we have is determined by the antigen on the blood cell surface and the antibodies that are in the blood plasma. Blood type A has A antigens, B blood type has B antigens, AB blood has both A and B antigens, and type O blood has neither.

Our bodies make antibodies against the blood antigens we don't carry on our blood. People with type A blood have antibodies against type B antigens, etcetera.

Let's define some terms. An antigen is any foreign substance that causes the immune system to produce antibodies against it. An antibody is a protein that can identify and defend the body against those foreign intruders. The intruder may be a chemical, bacteria, virus, or pollen.

An allele is one of a pair of genes that appear at a precise location on a particular chromosome and controls the same characteristic, such as color-blindness or blood type. The blood type that you and I have is determined by the alleles we get from our parents. The genes that control blood type in humans exist in three alleles, A, B, and O. Every child will receive one allele from each parent. From each parent, he or she will get an A marker, a B marker, or neither. A person only has type O blood if he or she got neither an A or B marker from either parent.

All this blood-type business is important when doing blood transfusions. For example, a person with blood type A will make antibodies against type B blood. If a type A person is given type B blood, the type A person's anti-Type B antibodies will cling to the antigens on type B blood cells, causing them to clump together and block blood flow. That's bad news for the cardiovascular system.

Anybody can donate blood to other people from his or her own blood group. In addition, type O blood donors can give to A, B and AB. Their blood has no antigens for the receiver's blood to attack. For this reason, people with type O blood are referred to as "universal donors." People with blood type AB have no anti-A or -B antibodies. They can receive blood from any other blood type and are referred to as "universal recipients."

The earliest classification of blood types was done by the Austrian doctor Karl Landsteiner in the early 1900s. Czech serologist Jan Janský is given credit for describing the four types in use today.

There is another level of complexity, known as the Rh, or Rhesus, factor. This antigen may or may not be present on the red blood cell surface. If the Rh factor is present, a person's blood type is referred to as Rh+(Rh-positive). If it is absent, they are Rh-(Rh-negative). Combining the ABO with the Rh factor blood groups leaves a total of eight possible blood types: A+, A-, B+, B-, AB+, AB-, O+, and O-.

What about this Rh-negative? About 85 percent of humans are Rh-positive. But if a woman who is Rh-negative and a man who is Rh-positive conceive a baby, there is the potential for a baby to have a health problem. The baby growing inside the Rh-negative mother may have Rh-positive blood, inherited from the father. Approximately half of the children born to an Rh-negative mother and Rh-positive father will be Rh-positive.

Rh incompatibility usually isn't a problem if it's the mother's first pregnancy because, unless there's some sort of abnormality, the fetus's blood does not normally enter the mother's circulatory system during the pregnancy.

However, during delivery, the mother's and baby's blood can intermingle. If this happens, the mother's body recognizes the Rh protein as a foreign substance and might begin making antibodies against the Rh proteins.

Rh antibodies are harmless until the mother's second or later pregnancies. If she is ever carrying another Rh-positive child, her anti-Rh antibodies will recognize the Rh proteins on the surface of the baby's blood cells as foreign. The anti-Rh antibodies pass into the baby's bloodstream and attack those cells. This can lead to swelling and rupture of the baby's red blood cells. A baby's blood count can get dangerously low in this condition, known as hemolytic Rh disease of the newborn.

In generations past, Rh incompatibility was a very serious problem. Today, when a woman with the potential to develop Rh incompatibility is pregnant, doctors give her a series of two Rh immune-globulin shots during her first pregnancy. The first shot is given around the 28th week of pregnancy and the second within 72 hours after giving birth. Rh immune-globulin sweeps up any Rh antigens that cross from the fetus or newborn to the mother. This essentially hides the antigens from the mother's immune system, preventing it from producing potentially dangerous Rh antibodies, thereby protecting both the current baby and any future ones.

When are blood transfusions used? Most often, they are used to replenish blood lost in an injury or operation. A person who weighs between 150 to 180 pounds (70 to 80 kilograms) has between 10 and 12 pints (5 and 6 liters) of blood. Lose more than 4 pints (2 liters) and this person is in danger of going into shock.

There are several different types of blood transfusions in addition to the typical loss-of-blood transfusion due to an accident. Red blood cells can be transfused into patients with an iron deficiency or anemia. Doing so increases the body's hemoglobin and iron levels, which in turn increases the amount of oxygen carried through the body.

A plasma transfusion might be given to a person with liver failure, serious burns, or infections. Such a transfusion can keep the person's blood pressure from falling too low.

A platelet transfusion is sometimes needed by those suffering from cancers, leukemia, or to counter the effects of chemotherapy treatment. Platelets help stop the body from bleeding.

As you can see, blood type can be a bit tricky. If you don't know your blood type, you might want to ask your doctor. It is usually tested when you are born and is often found in your medical records.

Q9: Why can't you tickle yourself?

Aristotle also wondered about that. Why it's impossible to tickle oneself is an intriguing puzzle. British neuroscientist Sarah-Jayne Blakemore, writing in *Scientific American* magazine, looks to the cerebellum for an answer:

"Our studies at University College London have shown that the cerebellum can predict sensations when your own movement causes them but not when someone else does. When you try to tickle yourself, the cerebellum predicts the sensation and this prediction is used to cancel the response of other brain areas to the tickle."

The cerebellum, the region located at the back of the brain, monitors our movements. It can distinguish between expected and unexpected sensations. An expected sensation would be the amount of pressure your fingers apply to your keyboard while typing. An unexpected sensation would be someone sneaking up behind you and tapping you on the shoulder. The brain hardly notices the sensation of typing, but it pays a lot of attention to someone tapping on your shoulder. The difference in reactions from expected to unexpected is a built-in response that probably developed in early human history to detect predators.

Two brain regions are involved in processing how tickling feels. The somatosensory cortex processes touch, and the anterior cingulate cortex processes pleasant information. Being tickled often makes a person laugh uncontrollably, especially if the tickling is unexpected.

Both regions are less active during self-tickling than they are during tickling performed by someone else, which helps to explains why it doesn't feel tickly and pleasant when you tickle yourself. It seems that novel sensations tickle, and sensations are not novel if you cause them. If we grab our sides in an attempt to tickle ourselves, our brain anticipates this contact from the hands and prepares itself for it. Free of the feeling of unease and panic, the body no longer responds the same way it does when someone else tickles us.

Scientists suggest that the feeling of being tickled is a natural defense. If spiders or bugs crawled on you, a natural defense reaction would be to jerk away. But this doesn't explain why certain spots are most ticklish—under the arms, above the knee, at the back of the neck, or on the bottom of the feet.

Clever British researchers have come up with a robotic tickler to tickle yourself. It has a remote-control arm with a piece of soft foam attached to a plastic rod controlled by a joystick. A person lies on his or her back with eyes closed. Because of the disconnect between the joystick and the foam-covered arm touching our body, our brain is being tricked into thinking it is someone else doing the tickling. Subjects have described the sensation as being the same as if someone else is tickling them.

Q10: *How do some viruses make us sick?*

A virus is a strange creature, indeed. It's a microscopic lifeform that contains either RNA or DNA but does not have all the proteins and structures needed to reproduce. For that reason, it needs a host to help it. That host can be us. Viruses survive inside us in huge numbers, and new ones are discovered on a regular basis.

Viruses come in many shapes, some round, some complicated like a geodesic dome, some irregular. They're too small to be seen through a normal microscope. There's even debate as to whether they're living or non-living, since they cannot make more viruses on their own.

Viruses need other cells to reproduce. They enter a cell and insert their genetic material into the cell's DNA. When the cell copies this DNA, it starts churning out more viruses, sort of a Trojan horse. Trillions of copies are made, exploding the cells of the victim.

These new virus particles go on to enter other cells. When enough cells are damaged, the host, which is you or me, can get sick.

Many viruses behave themselves inside us, causing no harm. Others go wild and get out of control, replicating nonstop. They overwhelm our cell mechanisms, disrupt normal cell function, and cause our organs to stop working.

Soon a virus war is going on. Our immune system releases antibodies against the virus if it can. White blood cells hunt down and kill both viruses and infected cells. Our body can produce interferon, a substance that stops viruses from reproducing. We humans can increase our body temperature to kill viruses.

Increased body temperature, or fever, is just one mechanism our immune system employs to fight the flu caused by a virus intruder. A runny nose traps the virus. Sneezing and coughing expel viruses. Fluid transporting immune system materials can build up in joint spaces, causing aches and pains.

What diseases are virus-related? Flu, colds, AIDS, chickenpox, Ebola, hepatitis, yellow fever, rabies, mumps, measles, rubella, polio, Zika, herpes, and smallpox.

Some viruses have an animal "reservoir" where they can hang out before they reach humans. Rabies can be found in bats, dogs, and foxes. West Nile virus comes from birds. Influenza passes through birds, pigs, or horses. Ebola probably originates in fruit bats. HIV was most likely passed to humans from chimps and monkeys.

Viruses are extremely difficult to attack with drugs. They adapt, modify, mutate, or evolve so quickly, they build up a resistance to a drug. Some antiviral drugs have been developed in the past decades. One successful drug, acyclovir, is effective against the herpes virus. Many of the others are focused against the HIV virus, which causes AIDS. These drugs do not cure an HIV infection but do stop the virus from multiplying so the disease cannot progress. The same kind of progress has been made against hepatitis C. Vaccination has been successful in eradicating smallpox. Polio and measles may not be far behind.

An epidemic is an outbreak of an infection in a community. A pandemic happens when there is a worldwide epidemic. In 1918, a flu pandemic killed around 100 million people around the world. An unusual aspect of this pandemic is that it killed healthy young adults rather than the weakened and elderly. HIV is considered a pandemic, as an estimated 35 million people are living with the disease.

There is some good news. Yes, viruses kill thousands of people every year. But learning about how viruses insert new genetic material into living cells may someday help us cure many cancers.

Q11: Why is poop brown?

I wanted to get the "straight poop" on this topic, so I talked to a health professional, consulted *Gray's Anatomy*, and looked up some stuff on WebMD.

There is no delicate way to put it; if you eat, you poop. Let's review the journey. When you eat, saliva in the mouth uses enzymes to break down the food. When food is swallowed, it travels down a soft and long pipe in the chest termed the esophagus, which leads to the stomach.

The stomach, shaped like the letter *J*, uses gastric acids to break down the food so the body can use it. Then the food moves into a long tube called the small intestine. Coiled back and forth, the small intestine is more than 20 feet (6 meters) long. Its job is to absorb nutrients and minerals from the food.

Leftover food waste moves into the large intestine, or colon. The colon is about 5 feet (1.5 meters) in length and about 3 inches (8 centimeters) in diameter, shorter but wider than the small intestine. Its task is to absorb water from the waste. Lastly, out through the anus, and hopefully, into the toilet. Typically, it's a three-day trip.

Brown is the normal color of poop. An orange-brown pigment called bilirubin is formed when iron in red blood cells in the liver and bone marrow breaks down. Bilirubin ends up in the intestine. Yellowish bile from the liver is also dumped into the first section of the small intestine.

If you mix a lot of different paint colors together, you get new and different colors. Red paint mixed with blue paint equals purple paint. In the body, orange-brown bilirubin mixed with yellowish bile equates to brown.

The more appropriate medical term for poop is *stool*. The color of poop (stool) can change depending on diet. Eat some beets, the stool may be purplish. Healthy green vegetables, like spinach or kale, may generate a greenish stool. Iron supplements may also produce a green stool. Some bacterial infections may cause a greenish poop.

The color, texture, and the frequency of stool can give information about the status of your health. If the stool is bright red, it could be a sign of internal bleeding in the lower part of the colon. A dark black stool could indicate dried blood in the stool. This can indicate bleeding in the upper part of the digestive tract, giving the blood time to dry. If the stool is black and tarry, that means rapid bleeding from the stomach: Get help. Yellow poop means there is lots of fat. Lots of mucus could indicate Crohn's disease—or nothing. Small in diameter or ribbon-like stool could indicate a partial obstruction.

Doctors have reported that patients become alarmed when they spot corn in the stool. They are actually seeing the outer yellow part, which is mostly cellulose and indigestible fiber or husk. The inside of the kernel will have been digested, as it is starch.

Poop (stool) has a distinctive odor. It stinks, when you come right down to it. There is a science to it. Bacteria produce sulfur-rich compounds. The associated gas is hydrogen sulfide, which smells bad.

In the end (pun intended), brown poop is a good sign of a relatively healthy individual. Finally, your doctor, not a science column, is the place to seek accurate information on any medical issue.

Q12: Can hair turn white overnight?
· ·

W e can find stories of hair turning white overnight in the historical record. Sir Thomas More was an English lawyer, author of the famed book *Utopia*, and the lord high chancellor of England. Thomas More opposed King Henry VIII's separation from the Catholic Church and the annulment of his marriage to Catherine of Aragon. He was found guilty of treason. It is recorded that the night before his execution by beheading, July 6, 1535, his hair turned snowy white.

Marie Antoinette, the queen of France, was tried and convicted of a bunch of crimes by French revolutionaries on the morning of October 16, 1793. They shaved her head and guillotined her shortly after noontime on the same day. Accounts of those in charge say her hair had turned white.

There are other tales of extreme fright or stress turning a person's hair suddenly gray or white overnight. There does seem to be one case in more modern times of natural hair color turning to white.

In October 1901, famed sharpshooter Annie Oakley was on the train that carried Buffalo Bill's Wild West show through rural Virginia. There was a sudden, violent crash as the train hit another head-on. Miraculously, none of the people aboard were killed, but about 100 of the show's horses died on impact. Annie Oakley's hair turned white following the accident, reportedly from the shock.

It is well documented that natural hair color can change over a time frame of weeks or months. Hormone changes from pregnancy or taking medications can make a person's hair turn grayish quickly.

Every hair follicle contains pigment cells called melanocytes. The melanocytes produce eumelanin, which is black or dark brown, and pheomelanin, which is reddish-yellow. The melanocytes pass the melanin to the cells that produce keratin, the chief protein in hair. When the keratin-producing cells (keratinocytes) die, they retain the coloring from the melanin.

When we first start to go gray, the melanocytes are still present, but they become less active. Less pigment is deposited into the hair so it appears lighter. As graying progresses, the melanocytes die off until there aren't any cells left to produce the color.

Chemical bleach in hair dyes can render melanin colorless. Exposure to ionizing radiation and certain drugs can do the same. Stress and fear or any extraordinary emotion can change the color of hair, but not in an instant. When melanocytes die, hair turns white at the roots, but it takes time for the white to grow to the ends of the hair. Those stories about Sir Thomas More and Marie Antoinette could be a stretch.

There is a medical condition termed *diffuse alopecia areata*, which can result in sudden hair loss. The biochemistry of alopecia isn't well understood, but in people who have a mix of dark and gray or white hair, the grayish or whitish hair is less likely to fall out. A person can appear to go gray in a matter of days or weeks as the colored strands are lost. The change can be dramatic.

It seems most all of us will get gray hair as we age. The age at which this happens is largely determined by genetics. We will probably get our first strands of gray around the same age as our parents and grandparents started to go gray.

However, we have some influence over the rate at which the graying progress occurs. Smoking is known to increase the rate of graying. Anemia, generally poor nutrition, insufficient B vitamins, and untreated thyroid conditions can also speed the rate of graying. Some autoimmune diseases can cause premature graying. Exercise can stave off some of the graying.

Still, some people who are perfectly healthy start going gray in their 20s.

Q13: Why do we have an appendix?

The appendix is a small, 2- to 4-inch (5- to 10-centimeter) pouch located near where the large and small intestines meet. It resembles a little, closed tube. The appendix produces mucus and contains lymphatic tissue, which is part of the immune system. It also contains bacteria. Doctors have debated the exact function of the organ for years. Removing the appendix causes no noticeable symptoms.

The appendix can become inflamed and painful, a condition called appendicitis. Medical people think this condition usually begins when the opening of the appendix becomes blocked, allowing the bacteria inside the appendix to multiply, spread, and infect the appendix wall.

Once the appendix is infected, the body mounts an immune response to fight off the infection, resulting in inflammation. If the appendicitis becomes severe, the appendix may rupture, spilling the infection throughout the abdomen. This is a very serious condition that can result in death. Emergency surgery on an infected appendix prevents this dangerous outcome.

If we can get along without an appendix, why does the body have one? There are a couple of schools of thought on this subject.

One popular theory is that the appendix does perform a function, but doctors just don't know precisely what it is. There is some evidence suggesting a slight increase in the occurrence of Crohn's disease, which affects the bowels, in people who have had their appendix removed. This may be because the appendix does perform some function in fighting this disease. A few years ago, researchers at Duke University developed an idea that the appendix is a "safe house" for good bacteria in case bad things happen to the digestive system.

In 2011, researchers at Winthrop University Hospital in Mineola, New York, concluded that the appendix served a useful function in patients infected with the dangerous bacterium *Clostridium difficile. C. difficile* often appears in sick people who have been treated with lots of antibiotics, and it is difficult to get rid of. In patients with an appendix, the C. difficile comes back 11 percent of the time, but in patients who have had their appendix removed, the recurrence of the bacteria is 48 percent. The researchers reached the same conclusion as the Duke study: The appendix shelters good bacteria for when the body's digestive system needs them most. That way, when the gut is affected by a bout of diarrhea, a big dose of antibiotics, or some other illness that cleans out the intestines, the good bacteria in the appendix can repopulate the digestive system and keep you healthy.

These hypotheses are based on a long-known fact—the appendix is home to immune system tissue called lymphoid tissue. Lymphoid tissue's function in the digestive system is to protect the gut against pathogens. Other parts of the digestive tract that have lymphoid tissue are the tonsils, esophagus, adenoids, and stomach. Up until these studies, though, it was never clear what purpose the lymphoid tissue served in the appendix.

The other popular theory is that the appendix is a vestigial organ, an organ that had a purpose at one time, but no longer does. Perhaps our bodies worked a little differently or the environment was different at some time in the distant past. The appendix may have been useful at a time when humans regularly dined on tree bark and needed an additional organ to break down the roughage. Maybe in the past, the appendix produced a lot of mucus that was important for helping digestion and preventing infection in the intestines. These days we have better, cleaner food. Perhaps our stomachs work better in the first stages of digestion than they used to.

Other organs or features whose usefulness has been questioned include wisdom teeth, tonsils, the thymus gland, the tail bone, the little toe, and even the gallbladder.

The gallbladder serves as a bridge between the liver (which produces bile necessary for the digestion of fats) and the small intestine, where digestion occurs. The gallbladder stores the bile and parcels it out as needed. If the gallbladder is removed, it doesn't impair the production of needed bile, only its concentration and timed release into the small intestine. Dilute bile merely oozes in continually. A person can function quite adequately without the gallbladder under normal conditions, but it's better to keep it if you can.

Q14: Why is exercise good for us?
. . . .

An excellent question, and one that is very important considering that we are living at a time of record levels of obesity, diabetes, joint problems, and heart disease. Here are the reasons why we should all exercise.

- Exercise keeps the weight off by burning up those calories. To lose weight, you must burn more calories than you consume. Regular exercise knocks off calories that would otherwise be stored as fat.

- Exercise keeps fat off. Dr. John Porcari, professor of exercise and sports medicine at the University of Wisconsin–

La Crosse, says, "Exercise keeps lost pounds off. About 90 percent of people who have lost weight and kept it off for a year do about an hour of physical activity a day."

- Exercise make you feel good. It may not feel so good at the time you are swimming, or running, or bicycling, or lifting weights. But after cooling down, perhaps after showering, you get a sense of accomplishment and a glow of well-being. We tend to overeat if we are bored, tired, stressed, or in a not-so-good mood. Vigorous exercise helps regulate mood. If we feel good about ourselves, we tend to resist more-than-ample portions.

- Belly fat is the most dangerous fat. It greatly increases a person's risk of heart disease and diabetes. Dr. Michele S. Olson, professor of exercise science at Auburn University, Montgomery, says, "Exercise is absolutely essential for dropping weight and maintaining weight loss." She continues, "It's the easiest way to beat the bulge, period. Regular moderate to high-intensity aerobic exercise has the greatest impact on reducing ab[dominal] fat, the dangerous fat that ups your risk of diabetes and heart disease."

- Exercise boosts metabolism by preserving muscle mass. You'll lose fat if you diet without exercising, but you'll also lose muscle, which means you'll burn fewer calories going forward. The more muscle you have, the higher your metabolism and the more calories you'll torch.

- Exercise lowers the levels of cortisol, a hormone that has been linked to belly fat. Women with the most cortisol in their system have a higher body mass index (BMI) and bigger bellies than those with moderate amounts of the hormone, a University of California at San Francisco study found.

- Exercise trims inches. The number on the scale doesn't tell the whole truth, says Jari Love, a certified personal trainer and fitness DVD star: "When you shed fat and gain muscle you may lose inches and drop sizes without losing actual pounds. For instance, if you gain 3 pounds (1.4 kilograms) of lean muscle and lose 4 pounds (1.8 kilograms) of fat, you've actually experienced a 7-pound (3.2-kilogram) improvement in your body condition, despite the scale only showing 1 pound (0.5 kilogram) of weight loss."

- Exercise creates a healthy chain reaction. Boston-based psychologist Dr. Eric Endlich says, "Healthy habits tend to cluster together. When people make positive changes, like getting more exercise, they tend to work on other health improvements as well, such as eating better. The result is weight loss."

- Exercise brings on the fun. Rock climbing is way more exciting than eating a celery stick. That's why it's easier to stay slim by being active than by maintaining a strict diet. "If you look at people who incorporate exercise successfully in their lives, they've found something they truly enjoy," says Dr. Nancy Snyderman.

- Exercise stops hunger. People who exercise and diet are actually less hungry than those who only diet, according to a study in the journal *Obesity*. Bonus: Your self-restraint is higher, too.

- Exercise increases energy. Regular physical activity increases stamina by boosting the body's production of energy-promoting neurotransmitters, studies show. That pep gives you even more motivation to get moving.

Chapter Two

All the Plants and Animals

Q15: Can animals sense an approaching storm?

Yes, some animals are very keen in sensing forthcoming storms or other natural phenomena such as earthquakes or tsunamis. There is evidence that some animals make better use of their existing five senses than humans.

In December 2004, a huge tidal wave hit Southeast Asia and killed 200,000 people. Almost no wild animals died, except those penned up in cages. Prior to a large tsunami that stuck Sri Lanka in 2005, elephants ran for higher ground, dogs did not go outside the house, and flamingos left their low-lying coastal breeding areas.

Just before the big earthquake and tsunami that slammed into Japan in March 2011, people reported that animals behaved erratically. Some animals tried to get to higher ground, while others became distressed and anxious.

The prevalent feeling among researchers is that some animals can detect earthquakes and earth tremors as they are happening, even from a long distance away. Animals are able to hear sounds that humans can't hear. Frequencies below the range of human hearing are termed infrasonic. Humans can't hear frequencies, tones, or pitches below about 20 cycles per second, or 20 hertz. Elephants can "hear" below 20 hertz. They hear through their big feet. Earthquake shockwaves and ocean waves occur at frequencies elephants can hear, but humans cannot.

Hurricanes produce large decreases in air pressure and water pressure. Sharks that were tagged with tracking sensors were observed to swim to deeper waters during Hurricane Charlie. Birds and bees are also sensitive to air pressure changes. They will cover their nests or hives in advance of a severe storm. Many people observe that birds will hunker down as a big storm is approaching.

In short, scientists believe that many animals are attuned to their environment and that very small changes in that environment will cause them to move to safer conditions.

Questions often come up regarding the ability of animals to predict weather patterns. Can the behavior of bears give any indication as to the severity of winter? Most researchers think the answer is no. What about the groundhog? Is Punxsutawney Phil accurate? Folklore claims that if the Pennsylvania furry rodent sees his shadow on February 2, there will be six more weeks of winter. If no shadow, it's an early spring. According to Stormfax Weather Almanac, Phil has been correct 39 percent of the time. Not a good record!

Lots of woolly bear caterpillars can be seen in late September and all through October. The ends of the woolly bear caterpillar are black, and the band in the middle is a brown-orange. Some people believe that the wider the middle brown-orange band, the milder the winter to come. Conversely, if the middle band is narrow, prepare for a long, harsh winter. These predictions, drawn from folklore, have not been confirmed!

Q16: Why do dogs bury their bones?

The bone-burying dog is reverting to the behavior of its ancient ancestors. Burying bones is a survival instinct learned thousands of years before wolves were domesticated and developed into dogs. Dogs hunted in packs, much like modern-day wolves. The dog pack would send out scouts in all directions searching for prey. When they found, cornered, and killed a large animal, the feast would begin. But more than likely, there would be leftovers.

The dog, being a smart animal, knew that it had to save up for the lean times when food was scarce. Jackals and hyenas wanted a piece of the action, as did large cats, such as pumas, mountain lions, cheetahs, or tigers. Fellow dogs in its pack also got hungry.

Dogs have strong paws for moving dirt. Dig a hole, put in bones, cover them up, and the dog has created a savings account for the future. The hidden bones' smell was masked by the earth, and the moist ground slowed spoilage. Its cache was safe from scavengers. Buried bones have some meat on them, and the marrow inside the bone was sufficient to sustain a hungry dog in lean times.

Today's well-fed canines are less likely to go back to their ancestor's old ways of stockpiling food. However, if it finds more food than it needs or if feeding times are irregular, Rover may be seen carrying food behind the couch, as that hoarding impulse is quite strong. He may never return to the stash, as new food magically appears in his feeding bowl. Rover may also hide plastic bones and other toys. He will occasionally take clothing and towels to line his bed. Old habits die hard!

Terriers are the breed most likely to dig and bury. They get their name from the Latin word *terra* or the French *terre*, meaning "earth." Scottish terriers go after moles and other underground vermin. Their turned-out feet permit them to efficiently shovel earth to the side.

The food-hoarding pooch is not the only animal that thinks ahead. Beavers collect and store piles of vegetation around their lodges in expectation of a cold winter. Leopards will drag their kill high up into trees where other animals can't intrude. Squirrels bury acorns and nuts in the ground and in tree hollows.

Q17: Why does a mosquito bite itch?
· ·

It's not the bite that itches, but our body's reaction. The mosquito uses her piercing needle proboscis to penetrate the outer layer of skin. I say "her" because only female mosquitoes bite.

Once the straw-like proboscis gets down through the epidermis, the mosquito searches for a blood vessel in the dermis layer underneath. She secretes a bit of saliva that contains an anticoagulant that keeps the blood flowing smoothly. She does not want her "soda straw" to clog up. When the bloodsucker is finished with her meal, she flies happily away but leaves behind that saliva.

Our marvelous immune system senses an invader and produces histamine to combat the foreign intruder. The histamine gets to the site of the attack and causes the blood vessels to swell. That's the source of the reddish bump, or wheal.

When the blood vessels expand, nearby nerves are irritated. That irritation is the source of the itching. This entire process takes time, so a person may not realize they've been bitten for an hour or two.

That itching can turn out to be a good thing. It tells us that we have been bitten. Mosquitoes carry some really bad stuff. In the United States, it can be encephalitis and the West Nile virus. In more tropical climates, malaria is the big concern, along with dengue, Zika, and chikungunya fever. The itch may be a clue to a potential cause if a person comes down with one of those maladies.

Some people develop immunity to mosquito bites and are not affected. On the other end of the spectrum are individuals who develop swelling of limbs. Benadryl, an antihistamine, is useful to ease symptoms, as is calamine lotion. Ice packs provide relief, and so does aloe, a cream used in many sunburn remedies.

Mosquitoes are most active at sunrise and sunset when the air is calm. Those flying syringes are lightweight creatures and can't operate when it is windy.

One of the huge obstacles to building the Panama Canal at the beginning of the 1900s was the prevalence of yellow fever and malaria caused by the mosquito in that tropical climate. The French had lost 22,000 workers in their attempt to build the canal decades before.

Colonel William Crawford Gorgas was appointed to solve the problem. Mosquitoes lay their eggs on the surface of standing water. When the larvae hatch, they live just below the water's surface, breathing through a siphon in their tails. Eliminate the standing water and you eliminate the mosquito. That is just what Colonel Gorgas's crews did, by draining swamps, filling some wetlands, and spraying standing pools. They also fumigated residences, quarantined infected individuals, and provided screened verandas as sleeping quarters.

By 1906, one year after the start of the eradication program, only one case of yellow fever was reported. In 1914, the year the construction was finished and the Panama Canal opened, there were no cases reported at all.

Q18: Where did the first tree come from?

The earth's earliest plants are believed to be ferns and mosses that were only a few inches tall. About 400 million years ago, during the Devonian Period, plants formed stems, grew taller, competed for air, and developed root systems, vascular growth, and secondary growth. Scientists believe that there was no single moment when trees started, but rather a slow-developing process over millions of years.

Trees are really quite sneaky. Most have no branches at the lowest levels. The object of the trunk is to raise the height of the branches that grow the leaf canopy. Any plant that has leaves sticking way up there can get more sunlight than its neighbors.

By branching, a tree can spread its leaves to cover more area, hence gather more sun. A tree also spaces its leaves to prevent the leaves from shading one another. Further, the tree shades its root area to suppress any competition.

Sunlight is everything to a tree. Through the process of photosynthesis, the tree uses energy from the sun plus water, carbon dioxide, and chlorophyll to manufacture sugars. Here's the chemistry: Six molecules of water plus six molecules of carbon dioxide produce one molecule of sugar plus six molecules of oxygen.

You've just got to love trees. They provide shade, of course. They hold the soil in place, preventing erosion. They provide nests for birds and squirrels. Trees provide sap for maple syrup along with wood for burning, building houses, or making paper. Trees give us fruit. Marvels of engineering, they transport water up hundreds of feet to their highest twigs by the process of capillary action.

One third of the United States is covered by trees. And one third of that is set aside in our National Parks and National Forests. We have more trees today than 70 years ago.

In the past, trees were not evenly distributed across the United States, and the same is true today. The New England states are covered with forests. But Lewis and Clark observed "a vast treeless prairie" in the present-day Dakotas. There were so few trees in parts of the Dakota states that the pioneers built their houses of sod.

Do visit Redwoods National Forest or Muir Woods, Sequoia, or Kings Canyon National Parks in California to see these largest trees. In Sequoia National Park, stand in awe of the largest tree on Earth, the General Sherman Tree.

Who cannot be moved by the poem "Trees," written by Joyce Kilmer? Kilmer was killed by a German sniper at the Second Battle of the Marne in 1918 at the age of 31. Here's the poem:

I think that I shall never see
A poem lovely as a tree.

A tree whose hungry mouth is prest,
Against the earth's sweet flowing breast;

A tree that looks at God all day
And lifts her leafy arms to pray;

A tree that may in Summer wear
A nest of robins in her hair;

Upon whose bosom snow has lain;
Who intimately lives with rain.

Poems are made by fools like me,
But only God can make a tree.

Q19: Why do trees have rings?

Tree rings can be seen on a stump or log when a tree is cut down. Each ring equals one year of growth. Counting the rings is one method of telling how old a tree is. Tree rings are more noticeable in northern climates where seasons change from hot to cold so there is a large change in growth speed through winter, spring, summer, and fall. Some trees in tropical regions don't appear to have tree rings at all.

Tree rings grow in the cambium layer that is right under the bark. The bark is pushed out while the tree is growing. New woody cells are laid down each year. The cells are the building blocks that produce new layers of wood. The lighter wood is known as the early wood, with lots of water present. This wood is laid down in the springtime. The darker, denser wood is added on in the summer and fall when less moisture is available. The growth rings are most easily seen in pine and spruce (conifers) and hardwoods such as oak, ash, and walnut.

Trees are some of the oldest living things on Earth, having been in existence for 350 million years. An individual bristle-cone pine can reach an age of 5,000 years. People in California have counted 3,000 rings on a few redwood trees.

Tree growth rings can tell scientists a lot about weather and climate, both recent and ancient. If a tree receives lots of water, sun, and space to grow, the ring will be thicker. Thinner rings indicate the tree is stressed and not receiving the resources needed for growth.

Tree rings can divulge secrets of drought, severe storms, temperatures, soil pH, carbon dioxide concentrations, attacks by insects, and disease. Tree rings are used to check the accuracy of radiocarbon dating. Growth rings can also be used to date the wood in old buildings, ships, and frames for paintings.

It makes sense that drought decreases tree growth, producing a narrower ring. If a tree is crowded by neighboring trees, there will be a series of narrow rings. If the rings are narrow on one side of the tree with wide rings on the other, the tree was crowded on the side of the tree where the rings were narrow. Fire scars suggest past forest fires. The number of annual rings between fire scars shows the period between fires. Certain scars can indicate insect infestations.

Counting tree rings was a pastime for the three Scheckel boys growing up on the Crawford County farm in the 1940s and 1950s. We cut big trees for logs to haul up to Vedvik's sawmill in Seneca. Limbs became fence posts and firewood. We felled those trees with a two-man crosscut saw, mind you. No chainsaw for the Scheckel boys!

We would guess the age of the tree before sawing, yell "timber" when it was ready to topple, then rush back to the stump to count the rings. No prize for the best guess, only bragging rights until the next tree fell.

You must read the chapter in Aldo Leopold's 1949 book, *Sand County Almanac*, which he wrote after guiding a two-man crosscut saw through his lightning-killed oak tree north of Baraboo on the Wisconsin River in the 1940s. As he and his family cut, Leopold reflected on events during the tree's 80-ring lifetime, roughly 1865 to 1945.

He wrote, "Fragrant little chips of history spewed from the saw cut and accumulated on the snow before each kneeling sawyer. Our saw was biting its way, stroke by stroke, decade by decade, into the chronology of a lifetime, written in the concentric annual rings of the good oak."

A final tidbit about tree rings. The Little Ice Age occurred from around 1300 to 1850, the worst period being from about 1645 to 1750. It brought such low temperatures to northern countries that crops grew poorly. Thousands, if not millions, died of starvation in Europe and worldwide. New York Harbor froze over and people walked from Manhattan to Staten Island. Two feet (61 centimeters) of snow fell in New England in June and July of 1816.

The Little Ice Age froze the Vikings out of Greenland. The spread of the plague, or Black Death, was accelerated during the Little Ice Age as crops failed, starvation was widespread, and people congregated in close quarters to ward off the cold.

The Little Ice Age triggered the bloody French Revolution of 1789. Two decades of poor cereal harvests, drought, cattle disease, and skyrocketing bread prices kindled unrest among peasants and the urban poor. Many expressed their desperation and resentment toward a regime that imposed heavy taxes, yet failed to provide relief, by striking, looting, and rioting.

The Little Ice Age was instrumental in destroying the 1588 Spanish Armada. The Armada's 130 ships were unsuccessful in attacking the British navy in the English Channel and were driven north by strong winds. They attempted to sail "over the top" of England, Scotland, and Ireland and return to Spain. Violent storms drove many ships into the west coast of Ireland. Only 67 of the original 130 ships made it safely back to Spain.

It was so cold throughout Europe that tree growth was stunted, resulting in unusually dense wood. It is this rare, dense wood that contributed to the beautiful tonal properties of violins made by Antonio Stradivari.

Q20: *Where do fossils come from?*

A fossil is what is left when a plant or animal dies. The plant or animal becomes trapped in sediments, and the sediments turn to rock. Vertebrate fossils come from animals with bones. Invertebrate fossils are from plants or animals that did not have bones.

When a plant or animal dies, it is usually eaten or just decomposes away. On rare occasions, the plant or animal is buried in sediment such as mud, and if conditions are right, they harden into fossils.

Fossils can be animal tracks, or leaves, or parts of animals, such as teeth or bones. A mold is the shape of a plant or animal.

When mud and minerals fill the mold and harden, scientists use the term cast. The cast has the same shape that the plant or animal had when it was living. An imprint is a mold that is extremely thin, such as a leaf or feather.

A fossil is not the actual bone or leaf. A fossil is made up of minerals that have hardened, and it has the same shape as the original object. Imagine if you took a quarter and pushed it down into some molding clay or Silly Putty. When you removed the quarter, you would see the impression of the quarter, but the quarter would not be there.

As the original animal or plant material decays, water and minerals seep into the empty space and harden. A fossil is born. That is why most fossils are formed in sedimentary rocks, rocks formed in layers by mineral deposits in water.

Most fossils are rather heavy, colored tan or light brown, and feel like rocks. Well, a fossil actually is a rock that has the shape of something that lived eons ago. Some fossils were tiny insects. Some fossils came from large dinosaurs. Some are skins, bone, teeth, eggs, nests, muscles, claws, and even footprints.

There is a special fossil that is preserved in amber. Amber is the sap of a tree. The amber flowed over the insect and hardened. The entire insect is preserved, not just the exoskeleton.

People who study fossils are called paleontologists. These scientists have methods to determine the age of the fossil. How deep the fossil is buried is a clue. The various layers of rock and materials of the earth's surface are fairly well known.

Paleontologists can use radioactive decay of certain elements, such as potassium, found in rocks. Carbon dating does not work very well because it decays too rapidly. Carbon-14 has a half-life of 5,700 years.

Fossils have been found on every continent on Earth. Some of the more fascinating fossils are those of dinosaur footprints. Scientists can estimate the size and weight of the dinosaur by the depth of the depression and the distance between the footprints.

They can deduce how the animal walked or ran.

The teeth of fossils tell something about the diet of a bygone animal. Flat teeth indicate a plant eater, whereas sharp teeth show a meat eater.

Petrified wood is a fossil in which all the living organic material has been slowly replaced by minerals. Wood has been transformed into stone. This process takes place in water and mud, free of oxygen, where the original plant material is preserved. Mineral rich water flows through the tissue, and the minerals replace the plant material. The process may take hundreds of years.

In the United States, petrified wood can be found in South Dakota, Washington State, and Yellowstone National Park. One of the best places to view it is the Petrified Forest National Park in Arizona.

Bad fossil joke:

What do you call a fossil that doesn't want to work? Lazy bones.

Q21: Why do dogs have black lips?

Dogs do have different skin colors that correspond with their hair color. Dog lips are not exclusively black; they may be brown, tan, reddish, or pink, depending on the color of the dog and the color of the skin in the lips. For most breeds, the nose will be the same color as the lips. For example, the golden retriever has both a brown nose and brown lips.

A dog with black and brown on its muzzle may have both black and brownish skin on its lips. That same idea goes for eyelids, and even the sclerae, the "whites of their eyes." Many dogs do not have white sclerae, but instead have pigment throughout the eye.

Black and other dark pigment protects the dog from ultraviolet solar radiation damage. Dogs don't have much hair around the mouth area compared to other parts of the body. The black or dark color prevents the dog from getting sunburn and the mouth from being dried out. Dog lips follow dog noses. Lips and noses are both made from the same kinds of mucous membrane cells.

Lip color is inherited. The gene for black pigment is dominant over the genes for all other pigments. Some dogs have a piebald pattern of non-pigmented areas alternating with pigmented areas. The chow chow has blue-colored lips. The depth of the pigmented cells in the mouth tissue gives rise to the bluish tint. The chowchow's tongue is also bluish.

That same skin-lips relationship extends to humans. Not all humans have pink lips. Their lip color corresponds to their skin color, which the makeup industry has exploited to its benefit in manufacturing lipstick for all skin tones.

Pets that have unpigmented skin in hairless areas like lips and eyelids are at greater risk of solar damage, just like fair-skinned people. They may need sunscreen or need to be kept out of prolonged strong sunlight. Sometimes owners even tattoo their pets' eyelids a darker color to reduce the risk of sunburn or skin cancer.

Melanoma is a particularly common and aggressive form of cancer in both pets and people. It arises from any melanin-producing cell that has turned cancerous. According to the Veterinary Cancer Center, melanoma is the most common tumor found in the mouth of dogs, and the second most common tumor found on the toes. Male dogs get more melanoma. Certain breeds seem to be especially susceptible, including Scottish terriers, cocker spaniels, Gordon setters, chow chows, and golden retrievers.

Melanomas are locally invasive tumors, often infiltrate deep into the bone (of the jaw or toe), and have a high rate of metastasis (spreading). A noticeable swelling in the mouth is the most common sign, along with increased salivation, weight loss, pain, inability to eat, dropping food from the mouth, and loose teeth. The affected masses may be pigmented (black) or pink to white in color.

Melanomas can be diagnosed with a fine needle aspiration and cytology. A small needle is inserted into the tumor and some cells are removed and examined under the microscope. Since the mouth is a very sensitive location, most animals need some mild sedation for a needle aspiration. When a tumor is located on the toe, sedation is typically not necessary.

Melanoma in dogs is treated the same as in humans: removal of the affected area, radiation, and chemotherapy, if the owner can afford it. The average survival time for untreated dogs is only a few months. Dogs with an oral melanoma that have surgery and radiation therapy followed by the Merial melanoma vaccine have an improved median survival time of about one and a half to two years. The FDA has recently approved a drug called Yervoy—a drug that "unblocks" the immune system and allows it to work better.

Q22: How do eggs develop in a chicken?

E gg development is a marvelous process. The chicken takes in raw materials such as grain, bugs, and seeds, and converts that food into a nicely formed egg, all in about 25 hours.

Chickens will eat almost anything. They have no teeth, so they need grit. Grit is small fine gravel or tiny stone chips that help chickens grind seeds in their stomach. Hens require lots of calcium to form the egg shells. Most people who raise chickens feed them oyster shell, a source of calcium carbonate.

A hen, unlike most animals, has only one usable ovary, located on the left side near the backbone. A female chick at the time of hatching has 4,000 tiny ova, or reproductive cells. In theory, a hen could lay 4,000 eggs over her lifetime. In actual practice, most lay a few more than 500 eggs.

Egg formation starts when a sac bursts open and an ovum is released. It is on its way through a 30-inch (76-centimeter) coiled and folded tube called an oviduct. If a sperm is present, fertilization takes place, and a baby chick will develop. If not, a nice table egg will be the result.

The oviduct has five distinct sections in which the inner and outer shell membranes are added, along with some water and mineral salts. Then the albumen (egg white) is secreted and layered around the yolk. Water is provided to make the outer white thinner. Then the shell material is formed and hardened. Pigment is supplied if the shell is brown. The egg is ready.

We mentioned that a hen will lay about 500 eggs in her lifetime. The count depends on breed, diet, health, and environment. Most hens have two productive years before they go into semi-retirement. We're talking about 250 eggs per year. Hens prefer long days of sunlight, so production drops off in the winter. Some egg farmers add artificial lighting in the early morning or late afternoon, tricking the ladies into producing.

Female baby chicks grow into pullets. A pullet will start laying eggs at about six months of age. The White Leghorn breed is a prolific layer and was favored by the Scheckel family out on Oak Grove Ridge near Seneca, Wisconsin. The California White lays up to 300 large white eggs per year. Large brown eggs come from the Rhode Island Reds, Rhode Island Whites, and Barred Rocks.

The US Department of Agriculture (USDA) sets the standards for the sale of eggs. Eggs are graded by size, based on weight per dozen. The most common size is "large," which also is the size specified for recipes. The weight of a "large" egg must be more than 2 ounces (57 grams) per egg. Still larger sizes include extra large and jumbo.

Eggs are high in vitamin D and protein and have less cholesterol than previously thought. Over the years, we have heard that "eggs are bad for you" and "eggs are good for you." Perhaps we should heed Aristotle's golden mean: "Everything in moderation."

Q23: Why do horses need shoes?

It's so they can get a table in a restaurant. Ever see those signs: No Shirt, No Shoes, No Service? Just a joke; horses need shoes for a good reason.

The ancient Romans were the first to put shoes on horses. They built paved, rock-hard roads across their empire. Without shoes, horses' hooves would split and crack on the hard surfaces. The first horseshoes used by the ancient Romans were made from straw and leather.

In the wild, horse hooves wear down as fast as they grow. When horses were domesticated, they had to carry riders or pull heavy loads. The added burden placed additional strain on the feet of horses. The ancient Romans discovered that their horses were wearing down their feet faster than their hooves could grow. Excessive wear can cause lameness.

Yes, horse hooves grow, just like our toenails and fingernails. Also, the hooves are elastic, expanding and contracting. A horse grows a complete new hoof in a year.

A person who fits and applies horseshoes is called a farrier.

A farrier trims the hoof and fits the shoe. Modern horseshoes are made of steel or aluminum. Steel horseshoes make it easier to fit the shoe to the hoof. Some farriers will heat the horseshoe in a hot fire and mold the shoe to the hoof. This brings up images of the village blacksmith. Modern farriers carry a large supply of different sizes and shapes of horseshoes, so the red-hot horseshoe being pounded into shapes is pretty much a scene from the past. Aluminum shoes are lighter and permit the horse to move with a freer, flowing gait. Racing horses are most often fitted with aluminum shoes.

The farrier uses nails to attach the horseshoe to the horse hoof. Nailing shoes on the horse's feet does not hurt them, unless the nail is placed improperly. The nails go through the tough part of the hoof, which is not living tissue. The hoof is made of a horn-like substance. Like our toenails and fingernails, hoof material does not contain blood vessels and nerves.

Some horseshoes are glued onto the hoof, so nails are not needed. When a horse is fitted with shoes, we say it is shod. Because their feet are always growing, horses need their feet trimmed and their shoes reset on a regular basis.

Henry Burden was issued a patent in 1835 for a horseshoe manufacturing machine that could make 60 horseshoes per hour.

The famous Budweiser Clydesdale horses are shod with shoes that weigh about 5 pounds (2.3 kilograms) and measure 20 inches (51 centimeters) from end to end. They wear a size 9, about the dimensions of a dinner plate. In addition to the shoe, a leather pad is fitted between the shoe and the horse's frog, or sole of the hoof. This helps cushion and protect the more vulnerable frog from being injured by any hazardous debris that may be on a road, like glass or metal. Each pad and shoe are exclusively shaped for each individual horse in order to obtain the perfect fit every time. After all, these are valuable horses. (Special thanks to the late Steven J. Doll, DVM.)

Q24: How did ants build a pile of dirt in my grandpa's backyard?
. . . .

I t's called an anthill and is made by an army of worker ants carrying bits of soil and debris in their jaws and putting them at the exit of the hill. If you watch carefully, you will see the ants drop the soil material slightly over the edge at the top of the hill so that it doesn't slide back down into the exit hole. Those clever devils!

An ant colony is called a formicary and is highly structured and organized. Every ant has a place in the scheme of things, a job to do in a highly structured social setting. There are three kinds of ants in the hill or colony.

First comes the queen. She lays thousands of eggs to ensure the survival of the colony. Once she reaches adulthood, her sole job is to lay eggs. She has wings but sheds those wings when she establishes a new nest. Some ant species have one queen per hive or hill, while other species may have more than one queen.

There are a huge number of sterile females, called workers. These are the ants we typically see. They forage for food, work on building the nest or hive, protect the community of ants, and care for the queen's offspring. The worker ants are mostly blind. They "see" by using chemicals, vibrations, and ultraviolet light. When out foraging, ants leave a chemical trail so that they know where they've been. Those female workers do not have any wings.They can't fly the coop, so to speak.

At various times of the year, a number of winged sexual males and females depart the nest in a nuptial flight. The males, their job done, all die shortly afterward. Most of the females die also, but a few survive to start new nests as queens.

Certain types or species of ants are unique. Fire ants, prevalent in the southeastern United States, are aggressive and have a painful sting. They inject a venom to disable their prey or enemy. For us humans, it is an aching sting that feels like one has been burned by fire, hence the name. Fire ants hang around moist areas but can withstand harsh conditions.

Army ants are always on the move and do not build permanent nests. Most ant species have individual scouts to find food sources, but army ants send out a leaderless group of foragers to detect and overwhelm the prey all at once. There is only one queen and she is wingless. Army ants will seek out and eat reptiles, birds, and small mammals.

Leafcutter ants can defoliate an area very quickly. The large female workers cut the leaves while guarded by even larger soldier ants. Smaller worker ants sit on the leaves and fend off any parasitic flies. The cut leaves are stacked underground in compost piles that nourish a species of fungus. The leafcutter ants use the fungus as food, because they cannot digest leaves.

Ant hills were great fun for the three Scheckel boys out on the Oak Grove Ridge farm a couple miles northwest of Seneca, Wisconsin, in Crawford County. We came across a 2-foot (61-centimeter) high ant hill in the Kettle Hollow pasture where we ran beef cattle in the summer. Phillip, Bob, and I prodded and stirred the hill, watching ants scurry in every which direction. We boys had great fun, but it must have seemed like the end of the world for the ants.

Do read Henry David Thoreau's account in Chapter 12 of his *Walden, or Life in the Woods*. His "Battle of the Ants" essay recounts his observations of two armies, one of red ants and the other of larger black ants, in a gigantic struggle for survival.

Thoreau did have a lot of time on his hands. He picked up a wood chip on which two red ants were engaged in mortal combat with a black ant. He took the chip into his cabin and placed it under an inverted tumbler on the windowsill. The battle raged on. After a half hour, Thoreau examined the combatants under a low-power microscope and observed massive damage. You will have to dig up Thoreau's essay to get all the gory details and read about the outcome of this life-and-death struggle. I don't want to give away the ending!

Q25: Why do we have cats as pets?

There sure are a lot of cats around. About 80 million pet cats live in the United States, outnumbering dogs three to one. Pet owners claim their cat is much easier to care for than a dog. They can leave their cat alone for a few days, go away, and not have the expense of a pet sitter.

John Bradshaw, a dog and cat expert from the University of Bristol, has studied cats and dogs for 20 years. He claims that dogs perceive their owners to be different from themselves. As soon as a dog sees a human, it changes its behavior.

Cats don't seem to do that, Bradshaw says. Cats do not change their behavior between interacting with humans or with other cats. Rubbing against our leg, putting their tail up in the air, sitting beside us, and grooming; it's the same with a human as with another cat.

A second cat in the household can cause a ruckus. Cats don't always play well with other cats, and the resultant stress can bring on dermatitis, cystitis (inflammation of the bladder), and improper urination. The most common reason cats are brought to a vet, other than for routine vaccinations and desexing, is for wounds sustained in fights with other cats. This is especially true for cats that roam outdoors and encounter other cats that are strangers.

Cats can be sociable, but not as much as dogs. Behaviorists tell us that cats are not as far in their progression along the domestication spectrum as dogs are. Unlike dogs, cats are not interested in pleasing their master. Contrary to much opinion, though, cats can be trained. If a cat is getting into places it shouldn't, such as climbing on a table, or clawing at the curtains, a water pistol can reset its thinking.

Domestic cats go way back, well more than 12,000 years, when people began to store food in the Middle East. Archaeologists found a cat that was buried with a human on Cyprus around 9500 BCE. Some Egyptian cats wore jewelry. The ancient Chinese used cats to keep down the rodent population getting into their grain supply.

Cats were not indigenous to the United States. The thinking is that cats came over from Europe on boats, the same ones carrying people. Ship captains housed cats to control the rodent population.

Fast-forward to modern times, and we know that many farmers like to keep cats around to minimize the mice population. The Scheckel farm always seemed to have a half-dozen cats patrolling the place. We had one calico-colored feline we simply called Cat, and she was a gopher hunter. Often in spring, summer, and fall, we would observe Cat carrying a gopher across the field or lawn. We would carefully take the gopher, cut off its tail, and give the gopher back to Cat. There was a nickel bounty on gophers (25 cents on moles). We would take our cache of tails and feet, stored in a salted jar, to the town treasurer once a year. He would pay the bounty. Why, you ask, was there a bounty on gophers and moles? Well, those varmints made tunnels that enhanced erosion of the soil.

Are black cats unlucky? That is one of those dumb superstitions that some people harbor. Yes, cats are uncanny, quiet, aloof, and may suddenly startle people. They can leap up on things that are three or four times their height. Cats have a reflective layer of cells (tapetum lucidum) in the back of the eye that helps them see in low light conditions. That layer acts like a mirror on the retina to reflect the light back through the eye. It gives the cat a second chance to absorb the light. We humans see cats' eyes "shine" at night.

Historically, the fear of black cats had a downside. In the Middle Ages, cats were persecuted along with witches. The bubonic plague was carried by fleas carried by rats. A robust cat population would have killed more rats. More cats, fewer flea-carrying rats, and more people surviving the deadly plague that destroyed one third the population of Europe.

Q26: Why do roosters crow?

R oosters crow in the morning to claim their territory. When it comes right down to it, they are saying, "Get out of my way and don't mess with my women, this is my coop." Most of the crowing takes place in the early morning because that is when birds are most active, and much of their territorial promotion takes place at that time.

Most of the vocalizations that take place throughout the day are for other types of communication, such as flock calling, which tends to keep members of a flock together. This is especially true if they are out of sight from one another. The crowing informs the hens that they should gather 'round. Another way of stating "I am still here, don't go straying over to Rooster B, the one with the really big red thing hanging down from his neck (wattle)."

The ladies (hens) love a rooster's wattle and comb that is big and bright. It is a sign of a healthy and robust rooster. Roosters use their wattle to attract potential mates. Hens commonly ignore roosters whose wattle is too small. Wattles are also important for controlling a rooster's body temperature, as the wattle has a healthy blood supply. During the summer, blood traveling through the wattle cools down before traveling to the rest of the body.

People who keep track of these things are called ornithologists (bird nerds). Japanese researchers at Nagoya University have run some tests on rooster crowing. They did find that roosters would crow at most any time of the day and in response to some stimulus, such as a car approaching, horn honking, or being fed.

They did all kinds of tests, such as keeping roosters in the dark for 12 hours, then in the light for 12 hours, repeating day after day. They tried a near dark scenario of several months. They tried tricking the birds by exposing them to bright lights and loud noises at various times.

They found that the roosters settled into a near circadian rhythm of a 24-hour internal body clock, much like humans. We've experienced rooster crowing at 3:30 or 4:00 a.m. This is consistent with the Japanese research. The roosters seem to anticipate light about two hours before the light appears. The rooster's internal clock takes priority over external prompts.

Another thing the scientists found was that the dominant rooster started crowing first. The lower-rank roosters waited patiently and followed the ranked rooster each morning. There seems to be a pecking order or crowing protocol. This observation further lends credence to the idea that crowing is a way of marking territory.

The crow of a rooster can be very loud. As a result, many cities ban backyard chickens. Some cities will allow layers (female hens), but not roosters.

Some of us who grew up on a farm love to hear a rooster crow. For me, it brings back fond memories of rural life out on Oak Grove Ridge in Crawford County in southwestern Wisconsin. Here are some chicken jokes that kids have told me:

Why did the chicken cross the playground? To get to the other slide!

How do chickens get strong? They egg-cersize!

What do you get if you cross a chicken with a cement mixer? A brick layer!

What do you call chickens crossing a road? Poultry in motion!

Q27: *Why do birds and butterflies leave for winter?*

Animals in a Wisconsin winter have three choices; hibernate, adapt, or migrate. Bears hibernate. They eat like mad all summer and get as fat as possible. They sleep a lot in the winter, when all body functions slow down. Frogs, chipmunks, woodchucks, and snakes also hibernate. Ladybugs seek out warm places, like our houses, and still hibernate all winter.

Some insects, like the woolly bear caterpillar, hibernate as larvae. Some moths hibernate as pupae. Still others, such as the mourning cloak butterfly, hibernate as adults. Others live up here in the north country as cocoons, eggs, or caterpillars. Come spring, they spread their wings and fly.

Animals can adapt to harsh winter conditions. Owls have adapted. Many change their color from brown to white. Their soft feathers allow them to be silent flyers. With keen vision and excellent hearing, they pounce down on field mice and voles.

Rabbit fur changes from brown to white. Rabbits will gnaw on leaves, bark, twigs, and moss and will seek shelter in holes in trees, usually below ground or beneath brush piles. Deer and squirrels stay active and scrounge for food all winter.

Wolves' fur grows thicker against the bitter cold. They're excellent hunters, eat well, but leave some of the food behind. The leftovers are gobbled up by other smaller animals. Eagles, coyotes, and other animals can survive winter because of wolves.

Still, many birds and butterflies migrate. Monarch butterflies spend the summer in Canada and the northern United States. They head for a better climate during the winter, migrating as far south as Mexico for the winter. Their annual migration across North America has been called "one of the most spectacular natural phenomena in the world." Monarch butterflies arrive to overwintering sites in coastal California or central Mexico around November. They start the return trip in March, arriving around July.

Most migrating insects go much shorter distances. In the western mountains, many animals just go down the mountain to where there is less snow and cold. Animals migrate to where the weather will be mild enough to make it easier to find food.

The American robin is the state bird of Wisconsin, Michigan, and Connecticut. Our Wisconsin robins head for Florida in the winter, same as many Wisconsin retirees. During the spring and summertime, there aren't many places in the state that you won't see a group of robins sitting together singing their beautiful song. Don't we all welcome robins as a first sign of spring?

Oddly, every winter a few robins stay in the northern states, surviving blizzards, ice storms, and nights as cold as -20°F (-29°C). Regardless of how cold it is on the outside of their feathers, their body temperature under the feathers is about 104°F (40°C). Their thick down feathers hold body heat in. They produce body heat by shivering. And they get the energy to shiver from their food.

Most of us think that these stay-behind robins are not the brightest birds in their species line-up. They just might be a few bricks short of a full load. The smart ones head south.

Q28: Why do giraffes have long necks?

The giraffe is a graceful and magnificent creature. A giraffe needs that long neck to reach the green juicy leaves at the tops of acacia trees. No other animal can reach that far up. The giraffe's long neck is a perfect adaptation to the animal's natural habitat.

At first glance, it may seem that each individual giraffe grew a long neck enabling it to reach high into the acacia tree. If fact, it was a gradual change in one or more traits over many centuries. Those traits, such as a long neck, enabled some individuals to survive and reproduce more successfully in their environment. That change took place in a large population of giraffes, leading to a gradual shift in neck length.

Over time certain individual giraffes just happened to have a slightly longer neck than their buddies. This allowed them to reach higher branches. Consequently, they reproduced more successfully, while giraffes of lesser stature perished due to competition.

The obvious question is: "Why didn't other animal species also adapt to be able to reach the succulent leaves?" That question has been debated for well more than 150 years. One answer is that animals adapt to different niches, specializing in different kinds of food. Other animals became grazers or browsers foraging on lower-growing bushes.

Giraffes can feed at a variety of levels, and the ability to browse up high in the tree during times of tough competition provided them with a big advantage.

Humans have seven cervical vertebrae, neck bones immediately below the skull. Amazingly, the giraffe has the same number of vertebrae in its neck, but each one can be about ten inches long.

Adult male giraffes top out at 19 feet (5.8 meters) in height, with a tongue that stretches another 18 inches (46 centimeters). Little wonder they can scarf down the highest foliage of an acacia tree that is 20 feet (6 meters) tall.

Giraffes, with legs splayed out, also munch on grass and shrubs. Males duke it out with other males with their long necks in competition for females, just like rams butting horns.

The giraffe's neck is unique. The cervical vertebrae are tied together in a ball-and-socket arrangement. It's the same sort of assembly that we humans have to connect our arm and shoulder. The joint between the neck and skull allows the giraffe to move its head almost perpendicular to the ground.

Vertebrae further down, the first two thoracic vertebrae also have a ball-and-socket setup. The thoracic vertebrae connect the neck vertebrae to the backbone. They permit extra neck flexibility. That lower swiveling ball-and-joint accounts for the hump we see on the back of the giraffe.

Giraffes have a complex pressure-regulation system in their necks that stops blood from rushing to their brains when they lower their heads. They have large hearts, tight skin around the legs, and a high concentration of red blood cells—all adaptations that help blood to circulate better. They have large lungs, enabling them to breathe at a slow rate. The air has a long way to travel.

Q29: Why do we find worms on the pavement after it rains?

Earthworms don't have lungs. They breathe through their skin and they need a balanced level of moisture to survive. Earthworms are unable to drown the way a human would, and they can even survive several days fully submerged in water.

When the soil is too dry, earthworms burrow deeper to find moisture. After a rainfall, the soil is wet, and they move closer to the surface. It is essential that worms live in a moist environment, so during drought conditions, life is certainly more difficult for a worm.

When there is adequate surface moisture or humidity, earthworms venture out above ground and look for new places to burrow. The wet weather of spring and fall seems to bring them out in droves.

Soil experts now think earthworms surface during rain storms for migration purposes. Dr. Chris Lowe, University of Central Lancashire in Preston, England, says, "It gives them an opportunity to move greater distances across the soil surface than they could tunneling through soil." He adds, "They cannot do this when it is dry because of their moisture requirements."

Another explanation for why earthworms emerge after rain suggests that raindrop vibrations on the soil surface sound like predator vibrations, specifically like moles. Earthworms often come to the surface to escape moles.

"Rain can set up vibrations on top of the soil like mole vibrations," says Professor Josef Görres of the University of Vermont's Department of Plant and Soil Science. "It is similar to how earthworms move upwards and out of the way when predator vibrations are felt. They could move in a similar way for rain vibrations."

Humans create vibrations when "grunting" for bait earthworms. To coax worms from their burrows, fishermen run a piece of steel or a hand saw across the top of a stake, which causes a rubbing sound to occur as the stake vibrates. Earthworms then move to the surface, much to the fisherman's delight.

Besides being good for fishing, earthworms are a good news story for gardeners. Geologists estimate that an acre of good black soil can hold up to a million worms. Makes your skin crawl! By building tunnels, earthworms help air penetrate the soil and circulate. They enrich the soil, move nutrients around, digest and break down organic matter, and improve drainage and soil texture. Earthworms do a good job of aerating the soil.

Earthworms are considered such beneficial creatures that most pest-control products have been designed not to harm them. There are currently no products specifically for controlling earthworms, and it's not recommended to try to kill them at all.

Earthworms use touch to communicate and interact, according to scientists who have performed experiments on earthworm swarms. If you come right down to it, they're touchy-feely creatures.

Q30: How do squirrels find the nuts and acorns they buried in the fall?

W e've all witnessed the squirrel's autumn ritual, their no-nonsense scurrying about the lawns and parks, front paws and cheeks full of acorns. They're preparing for winter.

In winter, a squirrel can stay hidden in a tree nest, hole, crevice, or ground burrow for a day or two, but after that they get mighty hungry and need to eat. Tree squirrels don't hibernate like their ground squirrel cousins.

Red squirrels collect their nuts and store them in piles. It's a central location, called a midden, located in a tree cavity, under leaves, or in branch forks of trees. The more numerous gray squirrels bury their nuts in the ground and in various scattered caches around their territory. Spreading the nuts around makes it harder for other animals or naughty squirrels to pilfer their entire food supply.

If a squirrel is scurrying all over the place and hiding nuts everywhere, how does it remember where the food is hidden? There have been two schools of thought on this subject. One theory is that the squirrel uses its sense of smell to find its stock of food. The second theory is that the squirrel has developed a mental picture, using landmarks such as trees.

The gray squirrel is a wily creature. It will bury "fake" nuts to trick other squirrels out of finding its stash. Some gray squirrels dig holes and bury nothing, pretending to have buried nuts.

Squirrels partly use scent to uncover their buried treasure, and they do steal a nut or two from other squirrels' caches. However, scent is not totally reliable. When the ground is too dry or covered too deep in snow, scent is of little use. Trying to find nuts through ice is impossible.

Scientists seem to study everything, and a Princeton group published a study in the journal *Animal Behavior* entitled "Grey Squirrels Remember the Locations of Buried Nuts."

The Princeton study indicates that squirrels use spatial memory to locate stored food. The squirrel goes back more often to its own food supply than to the caches of other squirrels. Squirrels bury their food near landmarks that aid them in remembering where they stored the food. They seem to form a cognitive map of all their storage locations.

They also remember the amount of food in their caches, returning first to the cache that has the largest amount of stored food. Some squirrels will dig up and rebury nuts to determine if the stored food is still good.

Dr. Peter Smallwood, at the University of Richmond, has studied squirrel behavior for 10 years. He says squirrels only find 75 percent of the nuts they bury, whether by smell or memory mapping. That's a bonus for the woodlands, because those unfound nuts can grow into trees.

Dr. Smallwood claims that a gray squirrel prefers to bury red oak acorns, which are rich in fat and sprout in the spring.

The squirrel is more likely to eat a white oak acorn immediately, because it will germinate soon after it hits the ground. The red oak acorn is high in tannin, which isn't as tasty as the white oak acorn. Mr. Squirrel will leave the red oak acorn for spring eating.

Spring is a hard time for squirrels. They're running out of stored food. They will go for road kills and Dumpsters with discarded pizza boxes and chicken bones. If desperate, they will seek out bird eggs and even young nestlings.

The fall season was always special for the three Scheckel boys growing up on the Crawford County farm outside Seneca. Fall meant squirrel hunting with the .22 single-shot rifle. We had to wait until we had the first frost—something about the meat not being good if the weather was warm.

We preferred the bigger red squirrels, but gray would do. Squirrels hid in their nests and leaves early in the fall season, but when the leaves were gone, they high-tailed it for holes in trees. We always kept a few firecrackers left over from the Fourth of July for our late fall forays.

Seeing a squirrel entering a hole, one of us would scramble up the tree, light a firecracker, and drop it down in the hole. More than a few times, that squirrel would come out, fur singed, head shaking. The squirrel was soon dispatched. We won't mention the time my brother fell out of a tree and broke his arm because the wind blew the firecracker back on him.

Our dad taught us how to skin a squirrel and prepare it for the frying pan. Squirrel is a very tasty, incredibly tender meat, same as rabbit.

Chapter Three

The Science of
Food and Drink

Q31: How are pumpkins grown commercially?

Pumpkins grown for pie filling and such are harvested mechanically. A machine that looks like a snowplow goes through the field, snips the pumpkins off the vines, and lines them up in a row. The pumpkins are left in the field a week or two to cure. Later, a tractor fitted with a conveyor belt moves through the field, picks up the pumpkins, and dumps them in a padded truck. Then it is off to the processing plant.

The pumpkins are washed in a disinfectant and then rinsed. Next, they are chopped into small pieces, cooked and mashed into a soft creamy paste, at the same time being sieved to remove pieces of skin, shell, or rind.

The pumpkins used for canning are not the kind of pumpkins we use for decorations and jack-o'-lanterns. Canning pumpkins are oblong and ripen to a dull tan brown color, not the orange color of Halloween fame.

Canning pumpkins have a very thin shell. The deep orange fleshy part is quite thick, and the hollow space inside is small. Just what one wants in canning a pumpkin: thin rind, thick pumpkin flesh, and no waste.

Today, a Libby's plant in Morton, Illinois processes 85 percent of the canned pumpkin in the United States. The plant can handle 500,000 pumpkins in a day. The seeds are sown in the spring, take 115 days from planting to harvesting, and need lots of sunshine. Libby prefers to process pumpkins that weight in at about 12 pounds (5.4 kilograms).

Pumpkins are fruit, same as tomatoes, cucumbers, green beans, and peppers. They are high in potassium and vitamin A. Today we often roast pumpkin seeds as a snack. Native Americans roasted strips of pumpkin over an open fire. They also flattened and dried strips of pumpkin rinds to make mats. At one time, people used pumpkins to cure snake bites and remove freckles.

Who does not enjoy watching a pumpkin soar through the clear blue sky? The record distance for "pumpkin chuckin'," using a medieval-type catapult or trebuchet, is around 2,000 feet (600 meters). Pumpkin cannons have shot an orange orb more than 5,000 feet (1,500 meters).

The record holders for growing the largest pumpkin are Tim and Susan Mathison of Napa, California, with a 2,032-pounder (921.7 kilograms). It took 105 days to go from seed to harvest. It is now on display at the New York Botanical Garden in the Bronx.

Q32: Why are cooking directions different at high altitude?

There is less air and hence less air pressure at higher altitudes, which means water boils at a lower temperature. Boiling occurs when water goes from a liquid state to a vapor or gas state. With less air pushing on the surface of the water, the water molecules find it easier to jump from a liquid to a vapor.

Water boils, changing from liquid to a vapor, at a temperature of 212°F (100°C) at sea level. Tomah, Wisconsin is about 1,000 feet (305 meters) above sea level. Sea level in the United States is defined as the level of the water at the Gulf of Mexico. The boiling temperature of water in Tomah is 210°F (99°C). Water boils at 203°F (95°C) at the Mile High City of Denver, Colorado. In Leadville, Colorado, the hottest the water can get is 194°F (90°C). On Pikes Peak, altitude of 14,114 feet (4,302 meters), water boils at 186°F (85°C).

Preparing food at high altitudes usually requires a longer cooking time to compensate for the reduced air pressure that lowers the boiling temperature. For baked items, such as cakes and pastries, it becomes a bit more complicated than just cooking longer. More water will evaporate (liquid to vapor) from the food, so the amount of water mixed with the food must be increased.

For expanding items like cakes, the reduced pressure will result in a larger volume, surpassing the ability of the cake cell walls to hold up. The cake will fall. Most cake recipes call for extra flour when baking above 3,500 feet (1,070 meters) altitude. Extra flour makes the cell walls thicker. Cakes will not brown as well under reduced pressure because of the lower boiling point of water. Higher oven temperatures or longer baking times are required.

Many recipes for baked goods include leavening agents such as baking soda or baking powder. The idea of a leavening agent is to produce carbon dioxide and cause the baked goods to rise. At high altitudes, gases expand more, so dough rises faster. Dough may need less rising time, and may require deflating, by poking, during the rising process.

Going to the top of Pikes Peak near Colorado Springs, Colorado, either by car or cog railroad should be on every American's bucket list. It is said to be un-American not to try one of the famous Pikes Peak doughnuts that have been served for almost a hundred years. They use a lot of flour in that recipe.

In 1893, Katharine Lee Bates, a 33-year-old English professor from Wellesley College in Massachusetts, took the train to Colorado to teach a summer English course. During that summer, Ms. Bates and other teachers hired a wagon to take them to the top of Pikes Peak. They covered the last few miles riding on mules. Katharine Lee Bates was so inspired by the view, she jotted down a poem, later set to music, known as "America the Beautiful." There is a bronze plaque on top of Pikes Peak commemorating her accomplishment.

Q33: *Can chocolate kill a dog?*
. . . .

Will your pooch flop over dead if it eats the ears off the chocolate Easter bunny? It depends. It depends on what kind of chocolate Rover scarfed down, how big Rover is, how much he ate, and Rover's breed. Chocolate contains theobromine. Theobromine is an alkaloid. In the same family as caffeine, it stimulates the central nervous system and cardiovascular system. You and I can process or metabolize theobromine quite easily, but for dogs that process is much slower. Large amounts of chocolate for a smaller dog, eaten rapidly, can be deadly. Toxic levels of theobromine can build up in the dog.

Small amounts of chocolate will give a dog an upset stomach, perhaps with vomiting and diarrhea. The next sign of theobromine poisoning from chocolate is hyperactivity such as panting, whining, and muscle twitching. While a big dog can tolerate some chocolate without any ill effects, large amounts of chocolate for any dog can bring on elevated blood pressure, irregular heartbeat, internal bleeding, muscle tremors, seizures, and a heart attack. It's the rapid heart rate that can deliver the fatal blow.

Not all chocolates are created equal. Cocoa, cooking chocolate, and dark chocolate contain the highest levels of theobromine. Milk chocolate and white chocolate have lower levels.

The usual treatment for theobromine poisoning is to induce vomiting as soon as possible. If you can get a few teaspoons of hydrogen peroxide down the affected pooch, that will induce vomiting. Hydrogen peroxide is cheap and available in any department store or drugstore.

Getting a dog to eat a small amount of activated charcoal can also be helpful. Theobromine binds to charcoal, which keeps it from entering the bloodstream. Activated charcoal is used in bar soap and in filters for fish aquariums. Keep Fido hydrated by providing plenty of water.

If you take the dog to the veterinary clinic, they will also try to induce vomiting. If the poisoning is serious, a vet can give a dog injections of anticonvulsants to control seizures.

All these problems can be avoided if people make sure that their dog does not have access to chocolate, keeping it in a high cupboard so the dog can't jump up and grab it. Giving chocolate to a little kid? Give him or her just a wee bit at a time so a begging or grabbing dog or generous tyke limits the amount any dog can ingest.

A few chocolate sayings: Chocolate makes everyone smile—even bankers. In the beginning, the Lord created chocolate, and he saw that it was good. Then he separated the light from the dark, and it was better.

Q34: How is olive oil made?

Olive oil is manufactured by crushing and pressing the fruit of olive trees. Olive oil is used in cosmetics, cooking, pharmaceuticals, and soaps. It is often also used as fuel in traditional oil lamps. Olive oil is graded according to quality, purity, taste, and aroma. Climate, soil, time of harvest, and the different variety of olive trees account for the olive oil properties of flavor, aroma, and color.

High-quality olive oil is obtained from the fruit of the olive tree solely by mechanical or other means that cause no alteration or deterioration of the oil. No heat, no chemical interactions, no solvents, and no radiation are used. The oil must not have been subjected to any treatment other than that of pressure, washing, and filtration. High-quality olive oil has an acidity between 1 and 2 percent.

The expensive highest-quality olive oils are cold-pressed, a chemical-free process that involves only cold pressure or cold centrifugation, which produces a natural level of low acidity. A highest-quality (extra virgin) oil must have an acidity of less than 1 percent. It has the best flavor and aroma among all kinds of olive oils and is used for salads, stews, soups, and other dishes. It is supposed to add a richness and subtle flavor to food that ordinary, semi-fine, or pure olive oil does not give. It is also supposed to be the most beneficial variety of olive oil for preventing heart disease and enhancing health with its antioxidant properties.

To enjoy their real flavor, high-quality olive oils are most often used raw in salads. Because of the time-consuming process required to manufacture these oils, the production volume is limited.

Olive oil is a mono-unsaturated fat, one that helps reduce bad cholesterol (LDL) in your blood, says mayoclinic.org. Replacing other fats in your diet with olive oil may help reduce your risk of coronary heart disease, obesity, and diabetes.

The time at which olives are picked can determine the quality and type of olive oil. Olives picked early in the season yield a fruity oil. Olives picked in the middle of the season yield an olive oil with a tart flavor, and olives harvested late in the season yield a gentle olive oil.

Olive oil has a shelf life of 12 to 18 months and does not need to be stored in the refrigerator. Shelf life can be extended by keeping olive oil away from heat and light in a closed container such as a dark glass bottle.

Look for the North American Olive Oil Association stamp/certification on the olive oil bottle to make sure it is the highest quality. Some olive oils labeled as being from other countries may have just been bottled there and made from olives not grown there.

Q35: Why does unhealthy food make me fat?
· ·

I t's true: Unhealthy foods can pack on the pounds. That eating too much fast food or unhealthy food leads to obesity seems fairly obvious. We put on weight when we consume more calories than we expend through physical activity.

The average person needs about 2,000 calories to go through a normal day's activities. Some people need a little more; some people need a bit less. It depends on the person's size, the action in the stomach, activity level, and metabolism.

When we eat and our body breaks carbohydrates down into glucose, the kind of sugar our body uses for fuel, the pancreas releases insulin to bring the blood sugar back down to normal. Insulin is a hormone that is best at turning extra fuel to fat. Processed foods generally supply us with simple carbohydrates that are easy to digest. Processed foods with simple carbs include grains like white flour in breads and dessert foods, white pasta, and short-grain white rice. These carbs break down into glucose quickly, so our blood sugar rises fast. To keep the blood sugar under control, the body releases insulin, usually more insulin than would be needed for higher-fiber, less-processed foods like whole fruits and vegetables or whole grains.

High levels of insulin moving around the body equals more "storage," usually in the form of fat. That is why diets that contain more fiber and moderate protein don't cause as much weight gain. Those foods don't cause the blood sugar to rise so high so fast, so there is less insulin released. The processed foods don't satisfy us long, because they are quickly digested, and the lingering high insulin levels lead us to feel hungry sooner. The blood sugar roller coaster ride can stimulate our hunger even though we have consumed ample calories.

Our metabolism and digestive system work in tandem to decide what portion of what we eat is needed for our daily activity. Those calories are used, but the extras go to our tummies and thighs, filling up our fat cells or even making new ones.

Today's processed foods are extraordinarily calorie-heavy compared to the food our ancestors ate—and incredibly cheap. A big slice of pizza, soda, garlic bread, and you're over 2,400 calories. That's just one meal, and a person is way beyond their "calorie limit" for the entire day. And for only a few bucks.

Some people believe that high calorie foods attract us more than other foods do because of the historic need to survive when there wasn't much food available. Starvation has been around since the dawn of man. It has exerted a strong selective pressure, favoring those who could quickly pack on fat in good times to last through the lean times. But today, aside from a few places on Earth, starvation is no longer our biggest problem.

We hear laments of school lunch folks who try to stem the tide of unhealthy foods. They will put out dishes loaded with fruits and vegetables that too many schoolchildren seem to ignore.

We should not overlook the genetic factors involved. There are some people who do all the right things and nonetheless have a hard time keeping trim and fit. Studies of identical twins separated at birth, indeed, show a strong genetic component to body weight. That is not to say that someone can be genetically doomed to becoming fat. Environment and behavior also matter a lot. It's just that different people have different metabolisms.

It may not be easy at times, but it does seem all those weight-loss gurus are on to something: Eat less and exercise more. As a population, we are not as active as we once were, so the body does not burn as much fuel. We aren't walking behind the horse-drawn plow, carrying buckets of water to wash clothes, or walking miles to school.

The weight loss industry is huge, upward of $20 billion per year. A dieter can choose from a whole array of salons, diets, programs, supplements, and pills. There is no lack of schemes and programs to separate dieters from their money.

Q36: How do home water purifiers work?
. . . .

Water purifiers have two goals. First, purifiers remove bad "bugs" like cryptosporidium and giardia. These parasites can lead to diarrhea and severe stomach cramps. Secondly, purifiers take out heavy metals such as lead, copper, mercury, and cadmium.

People purchase water filtering systems to provide safe and good-tasting water. They also want to save money by not buying bottled water. There are a myriad of water purifiers on the market. We'll examine two that are available in most department and hardware stores and that use differing methods.

Brita water filters turn regular tap water into filtered drinking water. Brita sells both a pitcher and a water faucet attachment that uses a porous block of activated carbon as the filtration system. Activated carbon is an all-purpose filtering system used for many industrial applications. Eventually, the charcoal's ability to filter maxes out at around 40 gallons (150 liters), and the filter must be replaced. If the filter is not replaced periodically, bacteria will grow in the filter. Brita gets rid of chlorine, lead, and mercury. It's a big seller.

The Kangen is another popular home unit. Kangen features a large easy-to-read display, has a high output rate, and is self-cleaning. It is a high-end item, and the unit can be quite pricey.

Tap water enters an antibacterial active-carbon filter that removes rust, lead, chlorine, and any muddiness. The important minerals of potassium, magnesium, and calcium are not removed.

The water then flows through a multi-electrode plate mechanism that ionizes the water and splits water into alkaline and acidic water. Sodium chloride and sodium hypochlorite solutions contribute additional ions to the water. These chemicals must be added to the unit on a regular basis. The operator can choose water to be slightly acidic or a bit alkaline. Kangen, like Brita, has cornered a good share of the water purifier market.

Larger, industrial water purification systems often use a system of reverse osmosis. Osmosis is a natural process. How does it work? Let's say we have two different concentrations of salt water separated by a membrane. Salt would a minor component (solute), and the major component (solvent) would be water. Water will go through the membrane from low salt concentration to high salt concentration. This will continue until the salt concentration is the same on both side of the membrane.

Reverse osmosis, as the name implies, is just the opposite. It is the process of forcing a solvent (water) from a region of high solute (salt) concentration though a membrane to a region of low solute (salt) concentration. This is done be applying a high pressure against the membrane. Reverse osmosis is another technique to provide clean drinking water for the home. Reverse osmosis systems have a long life and provide large quantities of water in very little time.

Reverse osmosis is a wonderful process, providing tons of fresh drinking water by desalting the sea. Since 1977, Cape Coral, Florida, has been receiving all its drinking water from the salty seawater of the Gulf of Mexico. At one point, the Cuban government cut off water and electricity to the US Naval Station Guantánamo Bay (Gitmo). Now the base gets its water from a desalination plant.

Astronauts on the lunar landing missions used carbon or charcoal filters to drink water coming from the fuel cells that produced electricity. Water coming from the fuel cells was so pure it did not have any taste. It is a good balance of minerals that gives water its taste. The astronauts preferred Tang orange juice to the spacecraft's water.

How much water should you drink? When I was a kid, the saying was eight glasses per day. Many health experts agree that we should be drinking enough water to keep ourselves properly hydrated, which means that our urine should be relatively clear and plentiful.

What does WebMD say? "All liquids help you stay hydrated. Water is usually the best choice, because it's free (if you're drinking tap water) and has no sugar or calories. But most healthy people can get enough fluid through the beverages they consume every day. These can include water, fruit juices, coffee, sodas, iced tea, and other drinks."

Mayo Clinic: "How much water should you drink each day? It's a simple question with no easy answer. Studies have produced varying recommendations over the years, but in truth, your water needs depend on many factors, including your health, how active you are and where you live."

In the United States, water delivered by public water supplies is regulated by the Environmental Protection Agency (EPA). Bottled water is regulated by the Food and Drug Administration (FDA). These two agencies have different standards for the water that they regulate. In general, EPA's quality standards are higher, because public water is sent out to a much larger number of people. However, FDA does have strict standards of purity and labeling that must be met by all manufacturers of bottled water.

Chapter Four

Remarkable People in Science

Q37: How did intelligence develop in humans?
. . . .

W hen the frontal lobe of the brain developed an estimated 100,000 years ago, it signaled a quantum leap in human adaptation and development. The functions of the frontal lobe allow us to grasp the consequences of our actions, to choose between good and bad decisions, to curb unacceptable social responses, and to filter differences and similarities between events and actions.

The frontal lobe is used to retain long-term memories. It allows us to recall events that happened months or decades ago. The frontal lobe is crucial for verbal and math skills. One could call the frontal lobe the CEO of the brain, because that is where the organizing and planning takes place. It's the part of the brain that allows us to think about our place in the universe. Scientists say that the frontal lobe is what separates man from beast.

It is a different matter when we ask these questions: Where does each individual receive their own intelligence? How much of our intelligence has been shaped by our genetics (nature) and how much by our experiences and the way we were brought up (nurture)?

This nature versus nurture question has been going on since the days of John Locke and René Descartes in the 1600s. Many scientists reach their conclusions by studying identical twins that have been separated at birth. These identical twins had the same genes (nature), but were reared in different families (nurture).

The Minnesota Twin Registry was started in 1983 to catalog and interview all identical and fraternal twins born between 1936 and 1955. Lately, they have added twins born from 1961 to 1964. It is a huge longitudinal study following these twins over many years, using questionnaires to probe their personality, interests, marital status, leadership abilities, finances, and substance abuse, to name a few.

The twin study has shown that identical twins raised apart show remarkable similarities in lifestyle, interest, attitudes, chosen professions, IQ, and just about every other facet of living. Their conclusion is that genes, not environment or upbringing, account for most of what we are.

The Minnesota Twin Family Study also concludes that environment does make an important contribution to intelligence differences throughout life, and especially in early childhood. Specifically, deprivation in early childhood can stunt the development of intelligence just as it can stunt physical growth.

Q38: Why do some people stay so healthy while others end up with an incurable disease?

No one knows the answer. How much of health and longevity is genetic, how much is lifestyle, and how much is environmental? Does plain old luck play a part?

The leading causes of deaths (in order) in America today are heart disease, cancer, stroke, respiratory disease, accidents, diabetes, and Alzheimer's. Heart disease and cancer account for almost two thirds of the total. However, for Americans under age 50, the current leading cause of death is drug overdose. This is certainly a preventable cause of death. Addiction is a disease, but avoiding opioids completely prevents the disease.

Lung cancer is still the number one cancer killer in the United States. We all recognize that most, though not all, lung cancers are related to smoking. And that certainly is preventable.

We have all known people who live healthy lives and come down with cancer of some kind. So what triggers those cancers?

Is it our food loaded with preservatives, or the harsh cleaning solutions we use, the air we breathe, or the cosmetics we put on? Some cancers, such as breast cancer and colorectal cancer, seem to run in families. There's that genetic component again.

There is good news on the cancer front. Changes in certain proteins, called biomarkers, have allowed earlier detection for lung, colon, breast, and prostate cancers.

Certainly, lifestyle is a big factor in staying healthy and in determining how long we live. There is general agreement that we as a people smoke too much, eat too much, eat the wrong stuff, and don't exercise enough. Lifestyle is more important now than ever before, considering the raucous debate over our current health care system.

Diabetes is a huge concern, especially type II or adult onset diabetes. Diet, weight, and lack of activity are cited as causal factors. Again, something we can control to a large extent.

A few years ago, Paul Harvey reported that our government commissioned a study to find out why people in Louisiana had a higher level of heart disease than the rest of the US population. Paul Harvey said on his broadcast, "Can you say deep-fried?" People who eat a lot of food that is cooked in certain kinds of oil have higher levels of heart disease.

As a teacher, I work with teens. They're a wonderful group, so vibrant, creative, and optimistic. The leading cause of death for teens is car crashes. Most all those dreadful diseases, such as cholera, smallpox, tuberculosis, influenza, diphtheria, typhus, anthrax, and scarlet fever, that took heavy tolls on youth and teens years ago, have been wiped out or controlled.

Q39: Why are Siamese twins born attached?

Conjoined twins is the medical term for Siamese twins. Conjoined twins occur once in every 200,000 births. The twins come from a single fertilized egg, so they are always the same sex and always identical.

The developing baby or embryo starts to split into identical twins within the first 15 days after conception. But for some reason, in conjoined twins, the process stops before it is completed. The partially separated egg develops into a conjoined fetus.

The birth of two connected babies is seldom easy. Half are stillborn, which means the babies are not alive when delivered. Only one third live longer than a day. The overall survival rate is about 15 to 20 percent.

If the conjoined babies have separate internal organs, the chance for separation by surgery is very good. Obviously, survival is not so good if the babies share vital organs such as heart, liver, kidneys, lungs, stomach, and intestines.

About 75 percent of Siamese twins are connected at the chest and upper abdomen area. About 20 percent are joined at the lower torso, sharing legs and hips. About 4 percent are connected at the head.

The term *Siamese twins* is derived from the most famous conjoined twins, Eng and Chang Bunker, who were born in Siam (modern-day Thailand) in 1811. They were conjoined at the sternum. They were exhibited in circus shows around the world and in the United States by P.T. Barnum.

In 1839, they decided to settle down and became farmers near Wilkesboro, North Carolina. They married two sisters. Chang fathered 12 children and Eng fathered 10 children. Eng and Chang died in 1874 at age 63. After their deaths, it was determined that they could have been successfully separated.

Q40: What does an astrophysicist do?
. . . .

An astronomer or astrophysicist is anyone who has ever looked up in the night sky, taken in the wonder of it all, and tried to figure out how it all works. An astrophysicist is fascinated by the moon, sun, stars, constellations, galaxies, nebulas, black holes, and the universe.

Astrophysicists work with computers, powerful telescopes, rock samples, star maps, satellites, robotics, and some very sophisticated high-tech instruments. They study, investigate, publish their findings, write reports, and give seminars to people in their profession.

Earth-bound astronomers and astrophysicists work with telescopes high in the mountains of the world, where the air is thin and cold, and the night sky is clear most of the year. They are away from city lights, pollution, and clouds. Astrophysics is funded by governments and universities. In the United States, most of the funding comes from the National Aeronautics and Space Administration (NASA).

Mauna Kea, in Hawaii, is home to the world's largest telescope (Keck), which uses two mirrors working together that are 33 feet (10 meters) in diameter. Located atop a dormant volcano, Mauna Kea has 13 telescopes operated by 11 countries. At an altitude of 13,800 feet (4,206 meters), Mauna Kea is above 40 percent of Earth's atmosphere. Other countries with big telescopes include Chile, Bolivia, Switzerland, and Russia.

Getting a telescope completely above the earth's atmosphere has tremendous advantages. The Hubble Space Telescope, launched into Earth orbit in 1990, is still going strong and has sent stunning photos of objects deep in space. Hubble could last through 2030 or even 2040, its performance overlapping with the next generation of space telescope, the James Webb Space Telescope, due to be launched from French Guiana on an Ariane 5 rocket in March of 2021.

James E. Webb was a NASA administrator during the time the United States was putting men on the moon. The main feature of the Webb Space Telescope is its mirror, which has a diameter of 21 feet (6.4 meters). Seventeen countries are collaborating on this project, whose purpose is to study the birth and development of galaxies and how stars and planets were formed.

Astronomers are very excited about the Webb Space Telescope. It will be placed at Lagrange Point L2, 1.5 million miles (2.4 million kilometers) from Earth and on the opposite side of the earth from the sun, a nice gravity-stable orbit. A Lagrange Point is a sort of parking place in space, a location where the gravity of two large objects like the earth and the sun can hold a third, smaller object in place.

Other Earth-orbiting space telescopes include the Spitzer (2003), Fermi Gamma Ray (2008), Herschel Infrared (2009), Planck (2009), and Kepler (2009).

Astrophysicists and astronomers are a neat bunch of people. Astrophysicists come from every country in the world and travel all over the world. They bicycle, climb mountains, make home-brew beer, run 10K races, play softball, watch movies, go white-water rafting, and attend concerts. Like other scientists, many play musical instruments.

The job market for astronomers and astrophysicists can be tight. But their job skills are easily transferred to the private sector, especially in the growing high-tech industries. The profession is evenly divided between men and women.

Want to be an astronomer or astrophysicist? Take lots of math and science and read everything you can about the skies, stars, planets, galaxies, black holes—all the stuff you find out there. I highly recommend the movie *Contact*, a 1997 movie starring Jodie Foster and Matthew McConaughey. Based on a book by astronomer Carl Sagan, *Contact* looks at what might be the scenario if we earthlings find evidence of extraterrestrial intelligence.

Q41: What do scientists do for fun?
. . . .

I t is no surprise that scientists enjoy the same recreational activities that the rest of us pursue. Their after-hour doings vary from the quiet hobby of stamp collecting to the rigors of mountain climbing. Here is a collection of accounts given by working scientists:

Colorado researcher: "As a scientist who's a mom, my fun time is generally schlepping the kids to soccer, lessons, etc., and then helping with homework, making dinner, etc. However, I bike-commute, and riding to and from work with the sun and the beautiful colors in the foliage has just been spectacular. I like to ride in the snow in the winter, because it's a challenge and fun, too. Sometimes I'll take a half day and ski, or take an extra-long route to work just to play a bit. I like to play piano. My daughter sings, so accompanying her as she practices is pretty fun, too."

Rice University scientist: "On the weekends, I go to our ranch where we raise cattle and horses. I love being able to see the stars in a dark sky and to listen to the coyotes and owls. My most fun hobby is going to solar eclipses. I'm leaving November 3 to go to Australia to the eclipse."

Solar research scientist: "I love to play music. I play the bagpipes with the Irish Pipers of San Francisco. This is something completely different to work, and the group I play with is very sociable. I also play softball with a group of friends in my local city once a week. I also really enjoy shopping and going for coffee on a sunny day or reading in the park. Most of all, I love to travel. I've been to many countries, but I've mostly traveled around the United States—I've visited 29 states so far! I'm originally from Ireland but now live in California, so one of my new hobbies is learning to ski. We don't get snow in Ireland, so this is a really exciting thing for me!"

University of Iowa professor: "I am learning how to grow orchids, and I am the newsletter editor for the Eastern Iowa Orchid Society. We have set up displays of our plants at orchid shows in Iowa, Illinois, Minnesota, and Wisconsin for many years. I am interested in movie special effects and film production, so I have volunteered on the screening committee for the Landlocked Film Festival, which brings filmmakers from around the United States and even from other countries to Iowa City, Iowa. I also like to read, so I regularly go to science fiction and fantasy book groups that meet nearby. I also love to travel. Sometimes I get to travel for work, but I also have been able to take trips to Europe."

These vignettes of scientists' free time depict choices that are quite common to people in all walks of life. What did some famous Nobel Prize–winning scientists do for fun?

Albert Einstein had a passion for playing the violin. Richard Feynman, who helped develop the atomic bomb at Los Alamos, played the bongo drums. Max Planck, founder of quantum physics, was a very good amateur pianist. Nikola Tesla fed the pigeons in the park every day. Marie Curie bicycled around France on her honeymoon with her husband, Pierre Curie. Erwin Schrödinger, famous nuclear pioneer, made miniature dollhouse furniture. Charles Darwin was an avid hiker and voracious reader.

Q42: *Who invented photography?*
. . . .

N o photograph of George Washington exists. There are many photos of Abraham Lincoln. Photography was invented between the death of Washington and the time that Lincoln became president. Before the invention of photography by Frenchman Louis Daguerre in 1838, people had to rely on artists for the likenesses of famous people.

Daguerre made his first photograph using a camera obscura, a box with a lens on one end and a ground glass plate on the opposite side, where the image was focused. The device was not new; Leonardo da Vinci described one before 1520. People used the camera obscura to trace objects and scenes by placing a thin sheet of paper over the glass plate.

What Daguerre did was invent a process to "fix" the image and preserve it essentially forever. He had been experimenting with silver salts that were known to be sensitive to the breaking down or decomposition by light.

Daguerre prepared plates of highly polished silver-plated copper and exposed them to iodine vapor. This produced a very thin layer of silver iodide on the surface. Using the camera obscura, he exposed these plates, producing a faint image. He tried many times and different ways to intensify the image.

One day, he placed an exposed plate, which had only a very faint image, in a cupboard that stored chemicals. He intended to clean the plate and use it again at another time. After several days, he removed the plate from the cupboard and found, to his amazement, a strong image on the surface.

Daguerre figured that one or more chemicals in the cupboard must have intensified the image. Day after day, he placed a silver iodide plate in the cabinet and, one by one, removed the chemicals. When all the chemicals had been removed, the image intensification still occurred.

Daguerre carefully inspected the cupboard and noticed a few drops of mercury from a broken thermometer on one of the shelves. He concluded that the vapor of the mercury was responsible for the intensified image. Daguerre proved it by experiment.

What we now call a daguerreotype was the result. Henceforth, photographers developed the faint latent image by placing an exposed plate over a cup of mercury heated to about 165°F (73.8°C). Unfortunately, many of those early daguerreotype workers suffered severe illness and early death due to the high toxicity of mercury vapor.

After the picture was developed on the plate, it needed to be "fixed," or made insensitive to more light. This was accomplished by removing the unaffected silver iodide with a heated and concentrated salt water solution. Later, hyposulfite of soda (sodium thiosulfate), commonly called hypo, was used instead.

Those early photographs required exposure times as long as 10 minutes. Portraits required the subject to remain very still for a considerable time. As the years passed, faster lenses and more sensitive chemicals were used. By 1860, a wet colloidal process was in use, producing a negative image on a glass plate. This process allows a person to make many copies from a single negative, instead of the one-time-only process of the Daguerre method.

Another advantage of the new process was getting rid of the expensive silver-copper plates and mercury fumes. Exposure time required just seconds. A disadvantage was that the whole process from taking the picture to developing had to be done in less than 10 minutes, so field equipment was needed, sort of a darkroom on wheels.

Best known of these early photographers is Mathew Brady, who opened a studio in New York in 1844. He took pictures of Andrew Jackson and John Quincy Adams. Brady went on the road during the Civil War with his horse-drawn studio and darkroom. He photographed thousands of war scenes, as well as politicians and generals on both sides of the conflict.

Q43: Are there any famous father-son duos in science?

I f you asked a dozen people what makes a life well lived, you would probably get a dozen different answers. To me it would be a life that contributes to the general well-being of people and to our planet Earth. Someone who followed the Golden Rule and did their best to follow the Ten Commandments could be said to have lived a good life.

Let's look to the scientific community for one example. William Lawrence Bragg (1890–1971) was an Australian-born British scientist who used X-rays to discover how matter is put together. His father, Sir William Henry Bragg, was a British-born scientist and mathematician, who graduated from Trinity College and won an appointment to a teaching post at the University of Adelaide in South Australia in 1885.

In 1889, Sir William Henry Bragg met and married a skilled watercolor painter, Gwendolen Todd. They had three children over the years, the oldest being William Lawrence Bragg, born in 1890. When young William Lawrence was growing up, his father experimented with the newly discovered X-rays. The way X-rays pass through a material can reveal its atomic structure.

When young Bragg broke his arm in a tricycle accident, the father X-rayed his son's arm. This was some years before X-rays were routinely used in the medical profession.

The family moved back from Australia to England in 1908, and young Bragg entered Trinity College, graduating with high honors in 1911. All the while he worked with his father, studying X-rays striking materials. Together, father and son were able to calculate the position of atoms in a crystal.

World War I interrupted the work of both father and son. Young Bragg was made an officer of the Royal Horse Artillery. He was assigned the task of developing a method for locating German artillery emplacements. He and his team set up an array of extremely sensitive microphones placed several miles apart. Their system was capable of accurately measuring the different sound wave arrival times between the microphones. By math triangulation techniques, they could pinpoint enemy gun positions to within 50 to 100 feet (15 to 31 meters). The sound ranging techniques made it possible to direct British artillery precisely onto German emplacements. For this work, Bragg was awarded the Military Cross and the Order of the British Empire.

On September 2, 1915, while engaged with German forces on the Western Front in France, William Lawrence Bragg received word that his brother had been killed in the ill-fated Gallipoli Campaign. A few days later, he received a message that both he and his father had been awarded the Nobel Prize in Physics. It was the first and only time in history that a father-son team won the prize.

After World War I, both Braggs returned to university teaching and research. In 1921, William Lawrence married Alice Hopkinson. They had four children. Alice Hopkinson was elected mayor of Cambridge in 1945 and served as the chairman of the National Marriage Guidance Council, among other roles.

The elder Bragg died in 1942, and his son worked on sound-ranging problems for the British Navy during World War II. After the war, William Lawrence Bragg ran the Cavendish Lab at Cambridge University and oversaw the work of Watson and Crick, who discovered the double-helix nature of DNA in 1953. William Lawrence earned every high scientific honor that can be bestowed on any scientist. In addition to his 1915 Nobel Prize, Bragg received both the Copley Medal and the Royal Medal of the Royal Society.

William Lawrence Bragg is just one example of a life well lived; as a dutiful son, who worked closely with his father, as a soldier who served his country in two world wars, and as a family man who married a person who was accomplished in her own right. They were parents of four successful children who made their parents proud. I recommend *William and Lawrence Bragg, Father and Son: The Most Extraordinary Collaboration in Science*, by John Jenkin.

Q44: Who invented the gun?

Like so much stuff we use in everyday life, the gun had no single inventor. It's a trail of improvements going back over 600 years. One early step was the Chinese invention of gunpowder before CE 1200. In 1250, the Franciscan monk, Roger Bacon, devised his own formula for gunpowder: a mixture of sulfur, charcoal, and saltpeter.

The first portable gun was essentially a hand cannon made from a strong metal tube, open at one end, with a hole drilled into the tube near the closed end. A soldier loaded gunpowder into the tube and rammed a ball or bullet down the barrel. Next, he stuffed some wadding down the barrel to keep the metal ball from falling out.

A fuse, or a bit of poured powder, was introduced into the drilled hole. When a soldier ignited the fuse, the gunpowder behind the ball turned into a gas. Gases take up a lot more space than solids. The expanding gases pushed the ball out of the open end of the barrel with great speed.

People started using hand cannons around 1430. Today, those hand cannons would be called pistols.

The blunderbuss, a gun associated with the Pilgrims, had a short barrel and flared muzzle. The widened barrel speeded loading and spread the shot. The ignition mechanism for a gun is called a lock, and many of these early guns used a matchlock. The matchlock had a slow-burning rope, which was ignited ahead of time, and then moved into position to light the gunpowder when desired. The rope glowed at night; rainy weather put it out.

The flintlock was a big breakthrough and became the standard for more than 300 years. Flint is a kind of rock. When flint strikes steel, the hot sparks of iron ignite the gunpowder. The flintlock was the soldier's main firearm during the Revolutionary War.

The percussion cap was perfected by the time of our Civil War in the early 1860s. The cap, about the size of a pencil eraser, was made of a chemical compound called mercuric fulminate, which is highly explosive. The cap fit over a nipple from which a tube extended to the powder waiting to be lit.

The cartridge came along near the end of the Civil War. The powder and bullet were enclosed in a metal shell with the powder sitting right behind the bullet. The powder was ignited by a sharp blow to either the rim or the center of the shell.

The phrase lock, stock, and barrel is a figure of speech meaning "all" or "everything." In a gun, the "lock" is used to hold ready the spark instrument. The "stock" is the part of the weapon held by the user. The "barrel" is the pipe that conveys the bullet. Collectively, they are the whole weapon, and therefore "everything."

It has been 213 years since the beginning of the Lewis and Clark Expedition to explore the lands acquired by the Louisiana Purchase. The 33 frontiersmen ran out of trading goods, whiskey, and food. But during their 28-month journey to the Pacific and back, the Corps of Discovery never ran out of weapons, bullets, and gunpowder.

Advancements in weaponry were inevitable. Rifling meant inscribing helical grooves in the barrel of a gun to impart a spin to the bullet in its path through the barrel. The gyroscope effect, much like the spin of a football pass, greatly improved accuracy.

The Gatling gun was the first rapid-firing weapon, a forerunner of the machine gun. The Union Army used Gatlings in the trenches during the siege of Petersburg, Virginia, in the last year of the Civil War from June 1864 to April 1865. The Gatling gun was a hand-crank-operated weapon with six barrels revolving around a central shaft.

A new, improved version of the Gatling gun, the machine gun, was employed by both sides in World War I. The machinery of war outpaced the tactics of the Great War, leading to devastating losses on both sides.

Q45: How do lightbulbs work?

T homas Alva Edison's 1879 invention of the lightbulb completely transformed the way we live and work. Imagine how hard it must have been to illuminate our world once the sun went down, using messy candles, torches, and oil lamps that tended to suck up the oxygen, soot up the room, and start disastrous fires. By 1900, millions of people around the world were turning on the lightbulb and turning off the dark. And amazingly, the lightbulb has not changed much in nearly 140 years.

The heart of the lightbulb is the tungsten filament. Tungsten is a metal that has an extremely high melting temperature of about 6,800°F (3,800°C). But even tungsten would catch on fire at such high temperatures. Fires need oxygen, so bulb makers take out the air inside the bulb. In other words, there is a vacuum (nothing) inside the bulb.

Those clever bulb-makers go one step further. They put a tinge of argon gas in the lightbulb. Argon is a big heavy atom. When atoms of tungsten evaporate off the filament, they run into argon atoms, which return the tungsten atoms right back onto the filament. The argon atoms act like bar-room bouncers.

Bulbs burn out when too much tungsten has evaporated away in one particular spot on the filament. The filament becomes thinner and weaker in that area. The filament is cold, you turn on the bulb, a heavy surge of current goes through that cold filament, and wham, a flash of light and the bulb is dead. We've all seen it.

The 1-inch (2.5-centimeter) filament in a typical bulb is more than 22 inches (56 centimeters) long. It is coiled, and the coil is made into a larger coil. Engineers discovered they could get more light per watt with this double coil method.

Lightbulb manufacturing is a marvelous example of compromise engineering, a compromise between bulb life vs. bulb efficiency. You could make a bulb last practically forever. Just make the filament really thick. But the bulb would be dim and consume lots of electricity. Not very efficient. On the other hand, you could make a bulb extremely efficient by making the filament thin. It would burn hot and bright and but last just a few hours.

Every bulb package is required to have three pieces of information on the label: wattage, life in hours, and light output in lumens. A 25-watt bulb will last about 2,500 hours, and a 100-watt bulb will last an average of 1,700 hours. The lower the wattage, the longer the life. That's because the filament is thicker on the low wattage bulb. But the 100-watt bulb is more efficient, which means you get more light per watt of electricity consumed.

A lightbulb in a fire station in Livermore, California, has been burning continuously since 1901. That 60-watt bulb is not very bright and not very efficient, but it illuminates the fire engines at night. It is a hand-blown bulb with a carbon filament that is eight times thicker than a modern lightbulb.

Many nations are phasing out the manufacture and sale of the time-honored incandescent bulb in favor of the more energy efficient compact fluorescent lamp (CFL) and light emitting diode (LED). Leaders in this movement include several South American countries and the European Union (EU).

Contrary to popular belief, the US Government never banned incandescent lightbulbs. Instead, our government established rules to mandate greater efficiency. It is difficult for a traditional incandescent bulb to meet those standards, but clever manufacturers have found a way around the rules by coming out with a halogen incandescent bulb.

Halogen will not kill the incandescent bulb, but the LED bulb might do the trick. LED bulbs are getting better by increasing their brightness and matching the color and texture of the beloved incandescent bulb. The cost of operating the LED bulb is extremely low.

The 2014 Nobel Prize in Physics was awarded to Japanese physicists Isamu Akasaki and Hiroshi Amano and Japanese-born American electronic engineer Shuji Nakamura from the University of California, Santa Barbara, for the invention of an efficient blue LED.

Red and green LEDs have been around for decades. With the additional of blue LEDs, we now have all three primary colors, red, green, and blue, needed to make white light. The long-lasting and efficient LEDs are revolutionizing the way we light the world.

Chapter Five

The Science of the Heavens and Earth

Q46: Why does lightning that is close give a sharp crack while lightning far away seems to rumble?

S ound is movement of air caused by a vibrating body. When lightning strikes, the air surrounding the path of the lightning bolt heats rapidly and expands explosively. Sound is created along the path of the bolt and moves outward.

As sound travels through air, the energy carried by the wave changes. Much of the energy of the wave is absorbed by the molecules of oxygen and nitrogen that constitute air. But the higher treble-like frequencies are absorbed more than the lower bass-like tones.

When lightning strikes close by, the sound travels a short distance through the air, so less absorption takes place. You hear all the pitches or frequencies, including a very strong mixture of those high frequencies that give that familiar sound of "cracking" electricity.

For lightning far away, the sound must travel through a long distance in air, with those high frequencies being removed or absorbed along the way. What is left by the time the sound gets to you are low frequencies, which have a "rumble" and "rolling" quality.

The hymn "How Great Thou Art" was originally a poem written by Carl Boberg, a member of the Swedish parliament in 1886, and set to a Swedish folk tune. Then the British missionary Stuart K. Hine wrote the English lyrics, which contains these lines: "I see the stars, I hear the rolling thunder." Why does thunder seem to "roll"?

A lightning bolt, a heavy surge of current, travels at about half the speed of light. Sound is created all along the path of the lightning discharge almost instantaneously. The lightning acts as a line source of sound, not a point source, such as would come out of a loudspeaker.

We, the observer and listener on the ground, are close to the bottom of the sound source and quite far away from the top of the path, which is usually up in the clouds. Even though the sound leaves all points on the path at the same time, it arrives at our ears at different times. We hear the sound from the bottom of the lightning bolt first, and then from points higher up. There is a prolonged rumble or roll of thunder as sound from different parts of the path reaches our ears.

To complicate matters even further, the lightning bolt path is seldom a straight line, but instead takes a tortuous, meandering, and jagged conduit.

How can you tell if lightning is about to strike? Lightning is caused by a tremendous build-up of static electricity. People about to be hit can feel the hair stand up on their body. They may feel a tingling sensation. On a smaller scale, it is like taking the clothes out of the dryer and separating a towel from a sock. You feel that static discharge. When that happens, get low on the ground and don't touch anything metal, like a golf club, fishing rod, ladder, flagpole, or tool you may be carrying. You do not want to experience this power. "Thy power throughout the Universe displayed."

Q47: What is lava made of?

The two most common elements in lava are silicon and oxygen. These two elements form a very strong bond. Other elements in lava are iron, aluminum, magnesium, calcium, sodium, potassium, phosphorus, and titanium.

Magma is the molten material beneath the earth's crust. Magma is made of rock, gases, and mineral crystals, all at 5,000°F

(2,800°C). Lava is the molten rock that comes out of a volcano or from a crack or fissure in the earth's surface. Lava is magma that has broken through the earth's surface.

The extremely hot lava is reddish in color and about 2,000°F (1,100°C). The temperature of lava is measured by metal probes called thermocouples. Lava flows like hot fudge being poured onto a plate. It moves slowly. You can easily outrun a lava flow. Hot lava from the Kilauea volcano on the Big Island of Hawaii during the 2018 eruption moved about 6 to 10 feet (2 to 3 meters) in a minute. The Leilani Estates saw a loss of 113 homes in the past few months. There is some good news. Island officials report that as of late August 2018, the eruptions and lava flow have virtually halted for the time being.

An awesome volcano adventure is a visit to Pompeii outside of Naples, Italy. Mount Vesuvius erupted in CE 79, and the ancient Roman town was buried under 10 to 20 feet (3 to 6 meters) of ash and pumice. It was lost for hundreds of years until it was accidentally discovered in 1748 by Spanish military engineers digging a new foundation for a palace.

Wonderfully excavated and restored, Pompeii is a UNESCO World Heritage Site that draws 3.5 million visitors per year. Streets, hitching posts, kitchens, artwork, buildings, and people are all preserved. Under the ash, everything remained as it was at the time of the eruption that killed 20,000 inhabitants. The eruption captured a moment in time.

Volcanoes do some good. They create new islands. For example, the Hawaiian Islands are volcanic. Volcanic ash is very fine, breaks down easily to mix with soil, and is rich in nutrients. Some of the richest soil on Earth is found on the slopes of past volcanoes in Indonesia, Japan, and the Philippines. Volcanoes help cool the earth by removing heat from the interior. Pumice is used as an abrasive in soaps and household cleaners. Other volcanic material is used for dams and concrete blocks. Volcanic basalt is used in road building, roofing granules, and concrete shields in nuclear reactors. The ancient Romans used pozzolana (volcanic ash) and lime to make the concrete that built an empire.

Q48: What is outer space made of?

The term *outer space* became popular with the start of the space age in the 1950s and 1960s. We can think of outer space as that large void that occupies the empty areas of the universe. Outer space is as close to a perfect vacuum, where there is nothing, as possible in nature. The temperature is close to absolute zero, or -460°F (-273°C). Whatever direction you look, it is inky black.

There is no clear boundary between our familiar Earth atmosphere and outer space because the air gradually thins the higher one goes. But by agreement with other countries in the 1967 Outer Space Treaty, outer space starts at 62 miles (100 kilometers) above the surface of the earth. Anyone can explore outer space freely for peaceful purposes. The United States recognizes any person going above 50 miles (80 kilometers) as an astronaut.

Outer space is not completely empty. There are a few hydrogen and helium atoms, neutrinos, dust, cosmic rays, and magnetic fields in this vast void. The absence of air makes outer space the ideal place to put a telescope. The Hubble Space Telescope, placed in Earth orbit in 1990, has sent back thousands of spectacular photos, some from the farthest reaches of the universe.

Objects in outer space may be beautiful, but living in outer space can be harsh and even deadly. Astronauts must wear a pressurized spacesuit if they are outside their spacecraft. If that spacesuit malfunctions or rips, the wearer will experience decompression. Their lungs will rupture, and the person will lose consciousness and die in minutes for lack of oxygen.

For short-duration flights of a year or less on the International Space Station, the human body takes a beating. Half of the astronauts get motion sickness, causing vomiting, nausea, headaches, and listlessness. Bones loses mass and muscles weaken. Changes take place to the astronauts' vision, their immune system, and their white blood cell count.

A trip to Mars, which is right next to us in our solar system, would take a minimum of three years. Our passengers would face the above difficulties, but in addition, radiation would bathe the entire body, and cells would be damaged. It will be a long time before we "boldly go where no man has gone before."

We mentioned that outer space is a vacuum. But getting a vacuum here on Earth was not easy, and when it first happened, it created a sensation. In 1640, Galileo was talking about a vacuum and knew that air had mass. It was his student, Evangelista Torricelli, using a mercury tube, who created a vacuum in 1643.

Torricelli took a 3.2-foot (1-meter) long tube and sealed it at one end. He filled the tube with mercury, capped it, inverted the tube, and set it vertically in a basin of mercury. The column of mercury fell to about 30 inches (76.2 centimeter), leaving a vacuum above. The column's height fluctuated with changing atmospheric pressure. It was the world's first barometer.

From France, Blaise Pascal figured that if air could support a column of mercury, that column should be shorter at a higher altitude. He talked his brother-in-law into carrying the mercury barometer to the top of a mountain, and sure enough, the column was shorter by 3 inches (7.6 centimeters). Soon, others conveyed a balloon up the mountain, noticing that the balloon gradually inflated, due to the lessened air pressure. Then on the way down, the balloon shrank again.

Q49: Which star is the biggest in the solar system?

The largest star, and indeed the only star in our solar system, is the sun. The sun is a bit under a million miles across. About 110 Earths put side by side would equal the diameter of the sun. The sun contains 99.8 percent of the mass of our solar system. It is 93 million miles (150 million kilometers) away, slightly closer on January 3 of every year, and farther away on July 5 of each year. Those two dates can vary by a couple of days.

The sun is an ordinary garden-variety class G star. Light from the sun takes around eight minutes to get to Earth. Nuclear fusion, converting hydrogen to helium, occurs in the sun with the release of a tremendous amount of energy.

The largest planet in our solar system is Jupiter. It is more massive than all the other planets combined. Jupiter is a giant ball of gas and liquid, spins faster than any other planet, and has an extremely strong magnetic field.

The largest moon in our solar system is Ganymede, a moon of Jupiter. Ganymede has over twice the mass of Earth's moon and is larger than the planet Mercury.

What about the largest star that we can see from Earth? That would be Sirius, a star in the constellation of Canis Major, the Big Dog. Sirius is a big, bright star, but it is also one of the closest stars to Earth. Sirius, also called the Dog Star, is 8.6 light-years away. A light-year is defined to be the distance light travels in one year, which is about 6 trillion miles (9.5 trillion kilometers) (a trillion is a number with 12 zeros; it equals a million million).

Sirius has twice the mass of our own sun and puts out 25 times the energy of our sun. Sirius has a companion star, a white dwarf star, appropriately called the Pup. It once was a mighty star but died out when all its hydrogen had been converted to helium.

The "dog days of summer," days of hot weather in late July and early August, were so named by both the ancient Greeks and Romans. At that time, Sirius rose in the early morning hours. That is no longer true, due to the precession of the equinoxes, a gradual shift in the orientation of the earth's axis of rotation, like what you see in the wobble of a spinning top.

Those ruthless ancient Romans would sacrifice a red dog in April just to appease the rage of Sirius, who they believed was the cause of the hot, humid weather to come.

How many stars can you see in the night sky with just the naked eye? About 2,000 on any one night, and about 6,000 over the course of a year.

One of the neatest tools for sky lovers is a cheap app for tablets and cell phones called Star Walk. There is both an Apple and Android version. It uses the tablet's GPS capability, no Internet connection needed. When you point the unit to the night sky, all the stars, constellations, planets, satellites, and galaxies are displayed and labeled.

Q50: How are galaxies made in the cosmos?

T his is what science says about how it all started. First, there was the big bang, that primeval explosion that brought all space, time, matter, and energy into being. For a long time, an estimated half billion (500 million) years, the universe was composed of a mixture of subatomic particles and radiation. The universe was too hot for elements to form.

As the universe cooled, the first hydrogen and helium atoms began to form. But exactly how those first elements formed into galaxies is not known. The most widely accepted theory is that there were small fluctuations or changes in the density of the universe in confined areas. Material started to condense into denser matter and attracted other gas and material, and these seeds become the first galaxies.

There is some tantalizing evidence. In 2007, the Keck Observatory telescopes found six star-forming galaxies at 13.2 billion light-years away. They were created when the universe was only 500 million years old.

Go outside on a clear moonless night, hopefully away from city lights, and you can see a hazy, luminous band stretching across the sky roughly oriented from the southwest to the northeast. You are looking edge-on into our own galaxy, the Milky Way. Galileo was the first to look at this band of light with his 30-power telescope. He found it was composed of countless dim stars.

Later telescopes showed that our Milky Way galaxy is just one of billions of galaxies that dot the universe, and that each galaxy contains billions of stars. Galaxies are not distributed evenly throughout the universe, but instead are found in clusters. Those clusters are parts of larger groups called super clusters. Astronomers don't know why.

While scientists are fairly clueless as to how galaxies started or came about, they do know quite a bit about what goes on in an individual galaxy, like our own Milky Way. They see stars in various stages. They see stars that are being born, young stars, middle-aged stars, and dying stars.

A few years ago, the Hubble Space Telescope was pointed at one tiny little speck of sky for ten days. Observers got the most detailed view of the early universe ever obtained. The Hubble photographed more than 1,500 galaxies in various stages of development, some dating back to the time when the universe was only a billion years old.

I do have an assignment for you. While you are out looking at the night sky, hopefully away from city lights, you will easily see the aforementioned Milky Way Galaxy. Realize that every star you see with the naked eye in the night sky is in our own Milky Way Galaxy.

There is one exception. There is a fuzzy little cotton-candy patch of light in the Andromeda Galaxy, off to the side of the giant square of Pegasus. It is listed as Messier 31 (M-31), the Andromeda Galaxy, a spiral galaxy like our own Milky Way. It is 2.5 million light-years away. The light you see tonight from that little fuzzy patch left the Andromeda Galaxy 2.5 million years ago.

As mentioned above, there are some cool apps that can turn your smartphone into a window on the night sky. Just point your phone at the night sky and your screen will show the stars, planets, and constellations. Google Sky Map is a free app for Android-powered mobile phones. Star Walk is marketed for both Apple and Android platforms.

Q51: How long does it take to travel to the moon?

Astronauts take almost three days to go from the Earth to the moon. The moon is 240,000 miles (386,000 kilometers) from the Earth, and the astronauts' spacecraft is going 25,000 miles (40,000 kilometers) per hour when they first start. However, gravity wants to pull the spacecraft back to Earth. As a result, it slows down. By the time it is close to the moon, it's only going about 3,000 miles (4,800 kilometers) per hour. Then, as the astronauts get closer to the moon, the gravitational pull of the moon increases their speed.

Twelve American astronauts have walked on the surface of the moon. They have brought back over 800 pounds (360 kilograms) of rocks and lunar samples for scientists to study. Thousands of years from now, people will think of this century as one in which man left the cradle of civilization and took that first big step. There is sound speculation that there will be tourists in Earth orbit within 10 years. It is not a far stretch of the imagination that people will go to the moon in 10 to 20 years.

A journey to Mars will take about eight months. Total round-trip time for a Mars odyssey would be three or four years, because you have to wait for the right time in the orbits of Mars and Earth to start a return journey. We will need a solid reason and a set purpose to go to Mars. The expenditure will be great and perhaps shared by several nations. Men and women may go to Mars during our lifetime, but a more realistic figure might be 80 to 100 years. A trip to the nearest stars will take thousands of years.

Try this experiment to give you a good idea of the relative size of the earth and moon and the distances between them. Wrap a string 10 times around a basketball. Hold the string at the center of the basketball and stretch the string across the room. Place a softball at the other end of the string. You now have an accurate model of the sizes and distances of the earth and moon. The basketball shows the size of the earth. The softball is the size of the moon. The string is the distance between the earth and moon.

Q52: What is meant by a blue moon?

A blue moon is the second full moon in the same month. This can only happen when the first full moon occurs near the beginning of the month, say the first or second day of the month. The time between any two full moons is close to 29.5 days. The second full moon will be on the 30th or the 31st of the same month. This only happens every two or three years. To be more precise, a blue moon occurs, on average, every 2.7 years. This gives rise to the expression "once in a blue moon," which means "very seldom."

There were two full moons in a single month in July 2015 and again in January 2018. The next one will be in October 2020.

The moon really does look bluish at times. It's due to dust, smoke, and oxygen particles in our atmosphere, not because it's the second full moon of the month. Large forest fires and volcanic eruptions will leave particles in the atmosphere for months, or even years. The result is a bluish tint to the moon.

The moon appeared bluish for two years after the 1883 Krakatoa volcano eruption. Shorter bluish periods occurred after the Mount St. Helens (1980) and Mount Pinatubo (1991) eruptions.

The moon is a wonderful object to view using common binoculars. Meteors, asteroids, and comets bombarded the moon for billions of years. The light-colored areas are the mountains or highlands. The dark-colored areas are the maria, or seas, formed later than the main bombardment, when molten lava from volcano and crater impacts filled in the lower basin areas.

I should point out that the British definition of a blue moon is different from our outlook here in the States. For the Brits, a blue moon is the third out of four full moons in a quarter of a year. A normal quarter is three months, so there should be only three full moons in a quarter. In summer season, the British call the first full moon the hay moon, the second the corn moon, and the third the harvest moon. If there is a fourth full moon in the summer quarter, they call the third one the blue moon, so the last full moon they can still properly call the harvest moon.

Just leave it to the Brits to add confusion. Aren't they the ones who drive on the wrong side of the road?

Q53: Why does the moon look really big when it comes up over the horizon but appear smaller when it is high in the sky?

The change in the moon's apparent size is strictly an illusion. There are several explanations for this illusion, which people have pondered for thousands of years. It makes sense that it is referred to as the "moon illusion."

Of course, the moon is not actually closer to the earth. The moon is about 240,000 miles (386,000 kilometers) from the earth, whether it is coming up over the horizon or whether it appears overhead.

The most commonly accepted explanation is that when we see the moon high in the sky, we have very little to compare its size to. But when the moon is on the horizon, it is behind trees, buildings, hills, etc. The moon seems huge compared to things around it. We see it being right behind an object we are comparing it to.

Another explanation of the "moon illusion" is the way we focus on close objects and faraway objects. When we look at the moon on the horizon, we focus on the moon at a great distance. When we look at the overhead moon, there are no visual clues to tell us how far away it is. We focus on the moon as if it were quite near.

So perhaps there is no right answer. Everyone can agree on one thing. The moon is the same distance away, whether we see it rising over the "The Great Pumpkin Patch" or whether it is directly overhead.

Try this experiment at home. Take a picture of the moon when it is at the horizon. Wait a few hours. Now, using the same settings, take another picture of the moon. Compare the sizes of the moon in the two pictures. You'll find that they are the same.

Q54: Will a balloon filled with air or helium float on the moon?

· ·

L et's consider a balloon filled with air and then a balloon a filled with helium. A balloon here on Earth filled with air sinks because the balloon and air inside weigh more than the air pushed out of the way (displaced) by the balloon.

We're using Archimedes' Principle, which determines whether an object sinks or floats. A balloon on Earth that is filled with helium (a very light gas) will rise or float because the balloon's weight, including the helium inside, weighs less than the air displaced. Put simply, the helium-filled balloon is less dense than air and will float upward.

Let's talk about a balloon on the moon. There is no air on the moon. Whether the balloon is filled with air or filled with helium, it won't float upward. For any balloon to stay aloft in any atmosphere, the gas inside must be lighter than the surrounding air. There is no air on the moon, so there is nothing for the balloon to rise above.

Let's say you fill a balloon with helium on the International Space Station. You let go of it. What will happen to it? Answer: It will just float in midair, same as if you let go of a hammer. The International Space Station, the balloon, the hammer, and the astronauts are all in free-fall.

Here are some facts about helium. Helium comes out of the ground along with natural gas. Helium is continually being made deep in the earth by the process of radioactivity. It is denser than hydrogen, the lightest of all gases. But helium is considered safe and will not explode. Hydrogen will blow up.

Imagine a birthday party for a four-year old, using hydrogen balloons instead of helium balloons. Consider all those lit birthday candles. That kid might not see his fifth birthday!

Q55: What are iridium flares?

Seen any strange lights in the night or morning sky? Have you spotted a bright point of light in the sky that looks like a star or planet and lasts from about three to ten seconds? You're not seeing a UFO. Rather, you have probably experienced an iridium flare sighting.

In May 1997, Motorola began putting up a series of 77 communication satellites. The system was termed *Iridium* because the atomic number of iridium is 77. The first generation of 66 satellites had three highly reflective aluminum antennas about the size of your front door. The sun at dawn and dusk reflects off these mirror-like antennas to our eyes on Earth. Computer programs have been developed to tell us where and when to look for such a reflection. Use this website: www.heavens-above.com.

The program asks you to type in your latitude and longitude. I use 43.9873°N and 90.4958°W for Tomah, Wisconsin. You get a list of iridium flares for your location and their relative brightness for the next seven days. The list tells you the time and direction in the sky to look to spot an iridium flare. Binoculars are nice to have once you've detected one.

It's a lot of fun to look for them, and sure enough, they appear exactly on time and precisely where the computer program says they are. People have reported seeing the brief light in the sky and believing they have seen a UFO.

The Heavens-Above Website also shows the current position of the International Space Station and the positions of the planets, comets, and asteroids. Throughout 2017 and 2018, the first generation of satellites are being replaced with a new generation that does not produce flares.

Q56: What is the proof that the earth orbits the sun?

It seems so obvious to us today in our modern times, but the earth orbiting the sun is a relatively new idea, only about 500 years old. Prior to about CE 1500, most of mankind held that the sun moved around the earth (geocentric model). The sun centered, or heliocentric, idea can be credited to Nicolaus Copernicus (1473–1543).

Is there a way that we can prove to ourselves that the earth indeed orbits the sun? Yes, there is, but it takes a year of patience and careful observation. Let's look at the *Astronomy Made Easy* or the *Astronomy for Dummies* books and see what they say.

Over the course of one year, the patterns of stars in the sky will change. On any particular night, some constellations of stars will appear on one side of the sky and others will appear on the other side. Those constellations of stars will disappear, and the original stars will return. The heavens rotate over the course of one year. It seems like the stars are set on a giant bowl and we are inside the center of that bowl.

But even though the stars look like they're attached to the inside of a giant bowl, most are at very different distances from Earth. Some are quite close, some are very far away, relatively speaking.

Over the course of one year, many of the stars will move relative to one another. Find two stars that are very close to each other. It's best if one star is slightly brighter or a different color than the other. It is possible to note, over a period of one year, that the two stars get closer to each other, seem to merge together, and then move apart. At the end of the year, they will be back where they started. This is because the earth moves around the sun in a near perfect circle, so that six months from your first observation, you are viewing the stars from a slightly, but observably, different angle.

This stellar parallax observation can only be explained if the earth is orbiting a "fixed" point, in this case, the sun. Simply put, parallax is the apparent change in position of objects due to a change in observation location. You can easily experience an example of parallax by holding your thumb out in front of your face at arm's length. Using just your left eye, look at where the thumb lines up with some object in the distant background such as a door frame or a tree outside. Now look with just your right eye. Notice the thumb moved. That's parallax, since your two eyes are at different locations.

The ancient peoples claimed that if the earth is moving around the sun then the stars should shift their positions due to this orbital motion. They should have been able to see this stellar parallax phenomena. In reality, they didn't see it, because the effect is very small, since the stars are so very far away.

Stellar parallax wasn't detected until 1838, and then only with a telescope, long after astronomers agreed the earth goes around the sun.

We amateur astronomers should probably just forget about picking out two stars in the nightly heavens and taking a year to observe their position. Yet, stellar parallax is still the best scientific proof we have that planet Earth orbits the sun.

Q57: Why doesn't Earth have more craters, like the moon?

Wherever we look in our solar system, whether it be by telescope or our fly-by satellites, we see craters on any of the rocky solid bodies. There are lots and lots of craters on the moon, Mercury, Venus, and Mars.

We don't see craters on Jupiter, Saturn, Uranus, and Neptune. They are gas giants, with no solid surface that can be seen. But their moons have craters, same as our moon. The craters are caused by meteor and asteroid impact.

There are craters on the earth, but most are blurred and hidden. The earth has features that no other planet in our solar system has: large oceans, much continental drift, and lots of life.

There are many unknowns about how the solar system formed. Scientists agree that a large disk of matter orbiting the sun slowly clumped into eight major planets (nine if you still count poor Pluto). But a small percentage of material formed into trillions of rocks, comets, and asteroids.

These objects move throughout the solar system in all sorts of wild orbits. Over a long period of time, thousands of these "rocks" will hit a planet or moon. In the earth's early history, the Late Heavy Bombardment, the number of impacts increased. The moon got hit really hard, creating many impacts that we see today on the moon. What about Earth? The earth got hit also. One of those was a large impact off Central America that killed off the dinosaurs. It's known as the Chicxulub Crater. If it had hit the moon, it would have created a nice big round crater we could admire with just a small telescope or good pair of binoculars.

So why can't we see that Chicxulub Crater? It's mostly under the ocean. The land part has been eroded by rain and wind and covered with jungle vegetation. The distinct round shape can best be seen using satellites and penetrating radar.

It is the same with other craters. Some 170 impact craters have been identified all over the earth. Some have lakes in the middle. Others are buried in sand dunes. Still others are obscured by jungles. Most meteorites hit in places now covered by oceans.

Over longs stretches of time, the plates of the earth have shifted and changed many surface features. Valleys open, mountains push up, coastlines rise and sink. That did not happen on the moon. Meteor impacts on the moon have remained intact.

There are some good-looking craters to be seen on Earth. The central Australian desert hosts the Wolf Creek Crater, 2,900 feet (880 meters) across and about 200 feet (60 meters) deep. The best place in the United States for crater viewing is at the Barringer Crater near Winslow, Arizona. Often referred to as Meteor Crater, it is 4,000 feet (1,200 meters) across and about 560 feet (170 meters) deep. The rim rises some 150 feet (46 meters) above the surrounding plain. There is a wonderful visitor center on the north rim and trails that lead around the entire perimeter and down into the bottom of the crater.

The best estimates place the time of impact for Meteor Crater at 50,000 years ago. Guesstimates place the impacting iron meteorite at 160 feet (49 meters) across with a weight of several hundred thousand tons. Impact speed is put at about 10 miles (16 kilometers) per second or 36,000 miles (58,000 kilometers) per hour. The energy of the impact was 2.5 megatons of TNT, equivalent to 125 Hiroshima-type atomic bombs.

Crater Lake in southern Oregon is another must-see natural attraction. However, Crater Lake is a remnant of a volcano, not created by meteor impact. It is the deepest lake in the United States, at almost 2,000 feet (600 meters) deep.

Chapter Six

Art, Music, Sports and Math

Q58: How many shades of red are there?

I read (pun intended) there are 285 shades of red ranging from alizarin to cerise to vermilion. A standard computer monitor shows 256 colors, of which about 20 can be categorized as red. The primary colors for printing are cyan, magenta, and yellow. Equal parts of magenta ink and yellow ink will yield a nice red.

Fire engine red is a bright intense red used on emergency vehicles, as the name implies. People expect their fire engines to be red. It's a long tradition. But many emergency vehicles are going with chartreuse yellow because of its greater visibility, especially at night. The neon yellow softballs used in high school sports and the road signs marking school zones are that same yellow-green color.

Red barns are another tradition out in the countryside. Several theories abound as to why barns are red. One theory states wealthy farmers added blood from slaughtered animals to the linseed oil used to preserve the wood. As the paint dried, it turned from a bright red to a darker, burnt red. Another theory suggests that farmers added ferrous oxide, or rust, to the oil mixture. Rust is a poison to many fungi, moss, and molds, which were known to grow on barns, where they would trap moisture and increase decay.

The British claim there are 285 shades of visibly different reds. It's hard to understand why the redcoats used that color in their uniforms during the Revolutionary War, when later the same red was used during deer season in our country.

Research indicates that women may be able to see more subtle shades of red than men. The gene that allows people to see color sits on the X chromosome. Women have two copies, and men have only one. The red gene swaps bits of genetic material with its neighbor on the X chromosome that controls the perception of the color green. Sometimes the exchange goes haywire and results in color-blindness. About 8 percent of men are color-blind. Few women are color-blind. Odds are that women will receive at least one good copy of the red and green genes.

My favorite red? Indian paintbrush, a wildflower seen when hiking the mountains of our National Parks in the American West.

Q59: Why is it easier to bicycle a mile than to run a mile?

I n both bicycling and running, the energy comes from the interior of the human body. That energy is derived from the food we eat. The difference between bicycling and running is our efficiency in transforming the potential energy of our muscles into the kinetic energy of motion.

Running is a less efficient means of transportation because the potential energy of the body is turned into internal energy of the ground and feet. The legs are moving up and down, starting and stopping during each stride.

Work done to accelerate the leg is transferred to the ground as the foot hits the ground and stops. Some of the energy of the foot is really heating up the ground slightly. That energy is not lost, but it is energy that does not propel a person forward.

In addition, when running, the body is moving up and down. The torso moving up and down slightly does nothing to make the person move forward. The arms are pumping when running. This takes added energy that also does not move the person forward.

In riding a bicycle, only the legs are moving. The motion is fairly uniform, as the feet move in continuous circles. Bicycling calls on the most powerful muscles in the body, which are the leg muscles. The body is utilizing other muscles, of course, but it is the leg muscles that are doing the heavy lifting (make that pedaling).

Bicycling is the most efficient of all means of transportation, including walking and running. One hundred calories of energy can power a bicyclist for 3 miles (4.8 kilometers), but it will make a car move only 280 feet (85.3 meters).

Efficiency is defined as the ratio of the work done by a machine, to the work supplied to it, expressed as a percentage. Stated another way, it is the output divided by the input. The efficiency of a bicycle is between 80 and 97 percent.

Most of the power in riding a bicycle goes into overcoming the aerodynamic drag force. This is the force of the body and bike running into air molecules and tends to slow the cyclist down. This aerodynamic drag increases with speed. The drag increases as the square of the speed, and the power required to overcome the added drag increases as the cube of the speed.

You go twice as fast, you have four times the drag. And it calls for two cubed, or eight times the power. Riding right behind another person decreases the drag. That's why, in bicycle races like the Tour de France, team members help "draft" for the team leader. They take turns riding in front and diverting some of the air molecules to decrease drag on the leader.

Bicycles are one of man's greatest inventions. Those old penny farthing high wheelers don't look too comfortable or safe. But the modern "safety" bicycle has not changed much in over a century. The basic drive mechanism, a large front sprocket driving a chain connected to a smaller sprocket on the rear hub, has been around for more than a hundred years.

Today, extremely lightweight frames are made of aluminum, carbon fibers, and titanium. Improved aerodynamic efficiency is achieved by streamlined frames and helmets. Tight-fitting synthetic clothing reduces "skin" friction. Electronic gear-shifting is showing up in high-end bicycles.

Q60: What math questions do kids wonder about?

· ·

To answer this question, I asked a fifth-grade teacher. She rattled off several popular questions, and this entry will deal with two: What is pi? What is infinity and how big is it?

Pi is a Greek letter (π), pronounced pie, that represents the ratio of the circumference of a circle (distance around) to its diameter (distance across). Pi is the same for all circles, no matter the size. Pi is called an infinite decimal, which means it just keeps going and the numbers don't repeat themselves. For practical purposes, use of 3.14159 for pi is close enough, and many would say 3.14 is good enough for pi.

Pi is also called an irrational number, which means it can't be expressed as a fraction. Pi shows up in all branches of math and science, trigonometry, geometry, statistics, mechanics, electricity, thermodynamics, cosmology, and dozens of scientific equations. People celebrate Pi day on March 14 of every year. Get it? 3-14.

There are folks who have memorized the value of pi out to 67,000 digits. These people have way too much time on their hands!

Infinity is rather abstract, theoretical, and hard to nail down. Infinity is not tangible, rather it is an idea. The symbol looks like the number eight lying on its side. Simply put, no matter how high you count, you can always count higher. Or no matter how far you extend parallel lines, they never can meet. Infinity is something that has no end.

It's like asking, what is the largest number? Well, there is no largest number, because you can always add a one to it. Infinity does not get larger, it is already fully created. Infinity is not a real number.

My two brothers and I would argue about this idea as kids on the farm when threshing, pitching manure, or milking cows. We applied it to the concept of eternity that we came across in our catechism class. Seems eternity and infinity were wrapped around notions of heaven and hell. We never did figure out or agree on how long eternity was supposed to be. We just gave up when our brains started to hurt. We did agree that eternity was a long time, and that heaven was preferable to that other place. My brother, Phillip, summed it up with "things that don't end" and we left it at that.

Some would say the size of our national debt and the amount of money spent on political campaigns is "infinity." Not so, it just seems that way. Others might contend that our universe extends to infinity. But we don't know how big our universe is. Perhaps we can leave it at this: Most things we know and deal with have an end, but infinity does not.

Q61: What are some additional math questions that make kids wonder?

The fifth-grade elementary teacher noted that students ask these additional questions: "Why can't you divide by zero?" "How do you know if a number is divisible by another number, without any remainder, before you do the division?" "What is a perfect number?" "What is a prime number?"

Dividing by zero doesn't give you an answer, so it is not allowed. Consider this: If we divide 8 candy bars among 4 people, each person gets 2 candy bars. What if we try to divide those 8 candy bars among 0 people, how many candy bars does each person get? We can't divide those 8 candy bars among 0 people, so the question really doesn't make sense. Mathematically, dividing by zero is said to be undefined.

As far as a number divisible by another number, there are certain rules. If the last digit of a number is even, the number is divisible by 2.

If the sum of the digits is divisible by 3, that number is also divisible by 3. Take 27 as an example. The sum of 2 and 7 is 9, and 9 is divisible by 3.

If the last two digits form a number that is divisible by 4, the number is divisible by 4. Use 124 as an example. The last two digits, 24, are divisible by 4, so 124 is divisibleby 4.

We just looked at the rules from 1 to 4, but there are rules that go well beyond 10, and they can be found on the Internet. Or it just might be easier to use a calculator.

A perfect number is a whole number (no remainders), such that if you add up all the factors (less than that number) you get that same number. Factors are any numbers that you can multiply together to get another number. One example of a perfect number is 6. Adding the factors of six (that is, $1 + 2 + 3$) gives you 6. A perfect number! Another example is 28: $1 + 2 + 4 + 7 + 14 = 28$.

The first four perfect numbers, 6, 28, 496, and 8,128, were known to the ancient Greek mathematicians. Those Pythagoreans gave mystical interpretation to these numbers. By the way, the fifth perfect number is 33,550,336 and was calculated in the year 1456 by some monk.

A prime number is one that can be divided evenly by 1 or itself, but nothing else. The first few prime numbers are 2, 3, 5, 7, 11, 13, 17, 19, 23, and 29. The number 4 is not a prime number, because it can be divided by 1, 2, and 4. The number 6 is not a prime number because it can be divided by 1, 2, 3, and 6. There are 168 prime numbers between 1 and 1,000.

An obvious question is: Who cares about prime numbers? Turns out that prime numbers are useful in designing machine tooling to reduce vibration caused by harmonics. To send and receive secure messages and information by cryptography and encryption makes extensive use of prime numbers. Prime numbers are used to encode information for credit cards and online banking. The design of metal grill racks in some of the newer microwave ovens utilizes prime numbers. No metal is supposed to be put in a microwave, but the spacing of the metal crossbars can be arranged so that the metal does not produce sparking or arcing.

Q62: What are mnemonics and how are they used in science?

Science instruction in our nation's schools is moving toward an inquiry-based, hands-on, problem-solving process. Massive research has shown that students do not achieve mastery of science skills and concepts by cookbook instruction and rote learning.

Yet, students do have some content items to memorize. The multiplication tables, for example, or procedures for word processing and lines of poetry. If students are going on to college, memorization skills are important.

Mnemonic devices are memory aids and have been used in the sciences for many years. Here is a partial list:

- ROY G. BIV: Red, orange, yellow, green, blue, indigo, and violet. These seven colors comprise what we call white light. Sir Isaac Newton named the seven colors that make up the rainbow. However, indigo is no longer considered to be one of the colors of the rainbow.

- My Very Educated Mother Just Served Us Nice Pizzas: These are the nine planets, starting from the sun, Mercury, Venus, Earth, Mars, Jupiter, Saturn, Uranus, Neptune, and Pluto. But Pluto is no longer considered a planet!

- PAW: Pour Acid into Water is the safe way to mix acid and water, not the other way around (WAP!)

- Kids Have Dropped Over Dead Converting Metrics: Prefixes to the metric system: Kilo (1000), Hecto (100), Deka (10), Origin (1), Deci (.1), Centi (.01), and Milli (.001)

- At the Commanding General's: Adenine, Thymine, Cytosine, and Guanine. These are the four nucleotides that make up the DNA structure of every living creature.

- King Phillip Claps Only For Great Students: Kingdom, Phylum, Class, Order, Family, Genus, and Species. This is the hierarchical classification system familiar to every biology student.

- Happy Henry Likes Beer But Could Not Obtain Four Nuts: Hydrogen, Helium, Lithium. Beryllium, Boron, Carbon, Nitrogen, Oxygen, Fluorine, Neon. The first 10 elements of the Periodic Table.

- The Strong Man's Triceps Explode: Troposphere, Stratosphere, Mesosphere, Thermosphere, Exosphere. The layers of our atmosphere heading outward from Earth.

- Camels Often Sit Down Carefully, Perhaps Their Joints Creak, Possible Early Oiling Might Prevent Premature Rheumatism. That's a mouthful: Cambrian, Ordovician, Silurian, Devonian, Carboniferous, Permian, Triassic, Jurassic, Cretaceous, Paleocene, Eocene, Oligocene, Miocene, Pliocene, Pleistocene, Recent. These are geological periods.

Larry Scheckel

Q63: How does throwing curveballs and sliders injure a pitcher's arm?

A curveball is thrown with "top-spin." At the top of the throwing arc, a pitcher snaps the arm and wrist in a downward motion. It's like turning a doorknob hard while throwing. It puts a lot of torque on the elbow.

The degree of break on the ball depends on how hard the pitcher can snap the throw and how much forward spin can be imparted to the ball. The harder the snap, the more the pitch will break downward. A typical curveball in the major leagues averages about 77 miles (123.9 kilometers) per hour.

Any breaking ball, such as the curveball or slider, employs the straightforward physics of the Magnus effect and Bernoulli's Principle. A topspin, for example, creates a higher pressure on the top of the ball, which deflects it downward.

A slider is a breaking fastball that tails sideways and down as it moves through the batter's strike zone. The slider is thrown with less speed than a fastball, but with greater speed than a curveball, sort of at an in-between speed. The average slider in the majors is about 84 miles (135.2 kilometers) per hour.

Throwing a slider is much like throwing a straight fastball. But the pitcher flicks his wrist inward just before the ball is released. The mechanics needed to throw a slider are more stringent than those necessary to execute a curveball. It requires a more violent arm motion. The ball is made to move to the side just as the batter is about to hit it. It's a wicked pitch that keeps batters awake at night.

Both the curveball and the slider can take a toll on a pitcher's arm. Much attention has been paid recently to the damage that these two pitches can do to young pitchers' arms and shoulders. The ligaments, elbow, biceps, and forearm muscles take a beating.

Overuse is the foremost cause of arm injuries to young baseball pitchers, whose muscles, ligaments, and bone are still developing. But throwing curveballs at any early age increases the risk, according to a huge study by the University of North Carolina.

Pitchers with a previous history of injury are at five times greater risk of elbow and shoulder injuries. The increase in risk is due to not getting enough rest, lack of medical treatment, skipping treatments such as icing, and taking too short a recovery time.

In the old days, some 20 years ago, we talked about innings pitched. These days, the conversation, and rules, center around the pitch count. Much criticism is reserved for kids' elite teams, the traveling or all-star teams. Elite pitchers might be playing on one or two regular teams, but they go on the road on weekends. The weekend teams often have different coaches from the kids' regular teams. Most of the time, the coaches are parents of one or two kids. The kids want to play, of course, so they are not always up front about how many innings or pitches they threw during the week. Twenty percent of pitchers throwing for traveling teams report arm pain, the study revealed.

On the positive side, most parents and coaches realize the dangers of arm misuse and overuse. Many won't allow a Little League pitcher to throw breaking stuff. Many leagues put in a pitch count limit.

It even happens at the major league level. In early April 2016, Dodger pitcher Ross Stripling had a no-hitter going into the eighth inning when Dodger manager Dave Roberts pulled him from the mound and put in a relief pitcher. Roberts received a lot of criticism, but Stripling's pitch count had reached 100, he never threw more than 78 pitches in spring training, it was his first time ever pitching in the majors, and he had missed all the 2014 season undergoing elbow ligament repair through the Tommy John surgery.

Just imagine, he was the first pitcher since 1892 on his way to throwing a no-hitter in his major league debut. But out of the dugout came "the hook," Manager Roberts had no apologies for taking Stripling out of the game, and most baseball people seemed to agree it was the prudent and right thing to do.

Manager Dave Roberts had met the parents of pitcher Ross Stripling at their hotel earlier that day and left 21 tickets for friends and family. A few minutes after taking Stripling out of the game, Manager Roberts was thrown out of the game for arguing balls and strikes with the umpire. San Francisco went on to beat the Dodgers 3–2 in 10innings.

Q64: What is the mathematics of the musical scale?

There is math in music, art, architecture, and almost every human endeavor. The math of music started with Pythagoras, a Greek born in the sixth century BCE. He is credited with the developing our understanding of the harmonic or overtone series. A plucked 2-foot (61-centimeter) string will vibrate at a certain tone or frequency, but a string that is 1-foot (30.5-centimeter) long will have twice the frequency. The two frequencies create an octave, a combination of notes whose frequencies are in a ratio of 2:1.

Music is constructed around intervals, the frequency ratio between two different tones. The ratio is found by dividing one tone's frequency by another. Our hearing is very sensitive to intervals, especially the ratio of 3:2, which is also called a fifth. The fifth is the interval between the two "twinkles" at the beginning of *Twinkle, twinkle, little star.*

The octave is divided into 12 equal half steps. Pythagoras loved the number 12. The frequency ratio for a half step is the 12th root of two, which turns out to be about 1.06.

What is meant by the 12th root of 2? We are familiar with the square root of 16, which is 4, because 4 times 4 is 16. The cube root of 27 is 3, since 3 times 3 times 3 yields 27. What number, multiplied by itself 12 times will give you 2? That number, carried out to the fourth decimal digit, is 1.0595. If we go with 1.06, that will be close enough.

If you take the note A above middle C, which is 440 hertz, and multiply it by 1.06, you get the next note, 466, which is B flat. Multiply 466 by 1.06 and you get a frequency of 493, which is the note B. All music is based on the 12th root of two. This 12th root of 2 rule is often referred to as the equal temperament system in which the frequency interval between every pair of adjacent notes has the same ratio.

Whether you are listening to Ricky Martin or Dean Martin, Beethoven or the Beatles, Queen or Prince, there is math in music.

Q65: *Why are Stradivarius violins so valuable?*
. . . .

A Stradivarius viola sold for a reported $45 million in 2014. That price tag broke the previous record of 2011 when a Strad violin brought the owner $11.5 million. The Stradivarius violin is perhaps the best known and most expensive of all violins. There isn't just one explanation but rather several factors that contribute to the value of these special instruments.

Stradivarius violins were made in the late 1600s and early 1700s by Antonio Stradivari, from his shop in Cremona, Italy. As a teenager, Antonio Stradivari served as an apprentice in the workshop of respected violin maker Nicolò Amati. Stradivari went on to set up his own business and quickly developed a reputation as a master of his trade.

Stradivari set about improving on the models produced by his teacher, Amati. The arches were altered, the color of the varnish was adjusted, and the thickness of the wood was modified, until Stradivari designed a model that satisfied his standards. Stradivarius violins are a complex blend of spruce and maple wood for the interior, strip, and neck. The wood was treated with gum and minerals, including potassium borate or borax.

Stradivari made a few more than 1,000 of the instruments, mostly for royalty and gentry. The number remaining today is believed to be about 650.

What makes a Strad so valuable and coveted? Foremost is the quality. A Stradivarius's value depends greatly on its condition. If the instrument is in excellent condition, the price continues to climb.

Modern instrument manufacturers have long strived to replicate the violin's timbre, but all have failed thus far. Musicians have long believed that a Stradivarius is superior to other violins in quality and sound. It's believed that cooler temperatures from the 1200s to the mid-1800s, a period known as the Little Ice Age, contributed to a denser wood, making the wood that was used in constructing the Stradivarius of a higher quality and offering a better acoustic output than the wood violin makers use today.

Second, there is the old-fashioned mechanism of supply and demand. One reason the value of a Stradivarius violin is so dear is because there are so few of them left, and they are no longer being made. Simple economics dictates that when there is a demand but little supply, value increases. The violins attract millions of dollars at auctions and are considered some of the most valuable artifacts in existence.

Third, a Strad is fashionable. Owning a Stradivarius violin is a status symbol in the world of music, thus increasing its legend, value, and price. It's like owning a Lamborghini, Bugatti, or Ferrari in the world of sports cars.

Stradivari didn't make only violins. He also produced violas (we mentioned one of them above), cellos, mandolins, and even a harp. His legacy lived on through his sons, who kept the family business going after his death.

Niccolò Paganini (1782–1840) claimed Stradivari used only "the wood of trees on which nightingales sang" and that affected the tonal quality. Despite modern technology, the techniques Stradivari used are yet to be fully understood or replicated.

Chapter Seven

Incredible
Technology

Q66: Why do some people put batteries in their refrigerator?

Most scientists and battery companies say that there is no advantage to putting batteries in the refrigerator. But as with many issues in life, there are some true believers. Batteries convert chemical energy into electrical energy. A chemical reaction taking place inside the battery generates electrons. The electrons sort of build up on the negative end of the battery, run through your flashlight bulb, and return to the positive end of the battery.

Most batteries in the past were carbon-zinc. Those older carbon-zinc materials would continue to react even when sitting on the shelf. The batteries ran down to some extent without being used. Today, most batteries are alkaline. The chemical reaction is quite different. The shelf life is greatly improved.

Extreme heat causes more battery damage than cold. Oxidation reactions, like those that cause rust, can take place inside a battery when it is very hot. Those reactions can use up the active ingredients in the battery. So, that myth about putting batteries in the fridge may have started in the days when air-conditioning was not widespread.

According to John Hadley, the technical service manager at Rayovac in Madison, Wisconsin, modern batteries can withstand temperatures up to 160°F (71.1°C) with little loss of power. The best place to store batteries, according to Hadley, is a cool, dry place. No need to put them in a refrigerator.

As an aside: The most common batteries that we use are the AA, AAA, C, D, and 9-volt. All of them are 1.5-volt batteries. If you take apart a 9-volt battery, you find six AAA cells wired in series. I discovered this tidbit by accident when I ran over a 9-volt battery with our car in the driveway.

Q67: How do elevators work?
. . . .

The concept of an elevator is quite simple. Tie a rope to a box, and you have yourself an elevator. Of course, a modern elevator must carry considerable weight and be safe at the same time. If that rope breaks, it's a bad day for someone!

Modern elevators use one of two systems, rope (cables) or hydraulics. Hydraulic elevators, such as the ones in two- or three-story buildings, use a fluid-driven piston mounted inside a cylinder. An electric motor pumps oil from a reservoir tank into a cylinder, and a piston is pushed up. The elevator sits on top of the piston.

When the elevator car gets to the correct floor, the pump is gradually shut off. As the elevator car descends, the hydraulic oil is allowed to flow back into the reservoir.

This system is identical to the lift your car rides atop when at a service garage, where they change the oil or work on the tires or engine. It is also like the small hydraulic jacks used to change a tire.

Hydraulic systems are limited to buildings that are only a few stories tall. The cylinder, with piston inside, is buried in the ground as deep as the building is tall. If the building is 10 stories tall, the hydraulic cylinder would have to go down into the ground 10 stories.

Another drawback to hydraulic systems is that they are not very efficient. Once the oil is drained backed into the reservoir, it needs to be pumped in again. There is no way to store the energy.

The most popular elevator system uses steel cables. The elevator car is raised and lowered with steel cables. The steel cable goes over the top of a grooved pulley called a sheave. When an electric motor turns the pulley sheave, the steel rope and elevator also move.

The steel cable that lifts the elevator car is connected to a counterweight. Most designs set the counterweight at slightly less than one-half the maximum capacity. If the elevator has a lift capacity of 4,000 pounds (1,800 kilograms), the counterweight is about 2,000 pounds (900 kilograms).

The purpose of the counterweight is to make it easier on the motor. The elevator car is on one side of the pulley and the counterweight is on the other side. It's like having a kid on each side of a teeter-totter or seesaw.

There are several safety systems on elevators. Elevators falling down shafts happen only in the movies. There are numerous steel cables, not just one. A governor system is built into the main top sheave pulley. If it rotates too fast, it shuts down. Electromagnetic safety brakes clamp on a rail if the elevator goes too fast or loses power.

Joke: What do you get if a piano falls down a coal shaft?

Answer: A flat minor.

Q68: What is the world's longest railroad?

The Trans-Siberian Railroad runs from Moscow to Vladivostok, a distance of 5,800 miles (9,300 kilometers). The trip takes seven days and crosses seven time zones. There are 9 tunnels and 140 bridges. The railroad has spur lines running into China through Mongolia and Manchuria and on into North Korea. Construction started in 1891 and finished in 1916. Convict labor was used to build the railroad. Crews started on either end, Moscow and Vladivostok, and built toward the center.

Vladivostok is important to the Russians. A warm water port is one that is ice-free year around, and Russia doesn't have many of those. Vladivostok, on the Pacific Ocean, is a warm-water port and home to the Russian Naval Pacific Fleet.

The Trans-Siberian Railroad crosses the famous Volga and Ob Rivers and the Ural Mountains that separate Europe and Asia. The railroad is credited with creating the cities of Novosibirsk and Omsk. Novosibirsk is a modern industrial and scientific research city of 1.5 million people.

Omsk, some 800 miles (1,300 kilometers) east of Moscow, was to be the Russian capital in the event the Germans overran Moscow in World War II. That did not happen, but Omsk became home to one of the factories that turned out the famed Russian T-34 battle tank. That T-34 tank was crucial in blunting German armor in the July 1943 Battle of Kursk. More than 6,000 tanks were involved in the greatest tank battle in history. Kursk was Germany's last hope of stopping Soviet forces moving toward Berlin.

The Trans-Siberian Railroad skirts the southern shore of Lake Baikal, the deepest lake in the world at 5,400 feet (1,600 meters) and the largest freshwater lake in Asia. Lake Baikal is a rift valley, where the earth's crust is pulled apart.

The Trans-Siberian Railroad uses a gauge of slightly less than 5 feet—specifically 4 feet 11 27/32 inches (152 centimeters) rather than the US gauge of 4 feet 8.5 inches (143.5 centimeters). The gauge is a measure of the distance between the rails.

The first American transcontinental railroad was 1,780 miles (2,865 kilometers) long. It was authorized by President Abraham Lincoln when he signed the Pacific Railroad Act of 1862. It was a war measure for the preservation of the Union. The Central Pacific Railroad started from San Francisco, California, and built eastward. The Union Pacific started at Council Bluffs, Iowa, and built westward. It was completed when the Golden Spike was driven in at Promontory Point, Utah, on May 10, 1869.

The book *Nothing Like It in the World*, released in the year 2000 and authored by Stephen Ambrose, is an excellent read regarding the transcontinental railroad. Ambrose was criticized for some factual errors in the book, but he does capture the gist and flavor of this magnificent achievement.

Q69: Why does a computer need to be rebooted?

Booting is defined as the process whereby a computer loads and runs an operating system (OS). The main purpose of a reboot is to perform an update process. Software installers and system software updaters often need to make changes to the core operating system files. They can't do that while the OS is in use without impacting its stability and the stability of programs that are already running. Rebooting lets the changes get done in a safe way without interfering with active tasks.

One key problem that existed in the past was the "leaking" of memory by poorly written applications. This would eventually cause a lack of available memory to the system, causing the paging of memory to disk, and hence a slowdown in the performance of the system.

Rebooting also has the advantage of letting the system security processes monitor changes to system files to make sure that unauthorized changes are not being made. Smartphones and tablets also need rebooting from time to time.

There probably is no end in sight for the reboot process. Rebooting in Microsoft's Windows 10 is much speedier than past versions. Microsoft added the welcome feature of a message popping up that reads something like "Installing update 1 of 4." The message lets the computer user know what's going on.

When new software is being installed, a Dynamic Link Library (DLL), which is used by lots of other software packages, needs to be updated to a new version. That DLL is a file that has instructions that other programs can call upon to do certain tasks.

Sometimes the instructions for a new software application, such as Microsoft Office Suite, will ask you to close all other programs before installing the new stuff. If the DLL is being used by an already running application, part of it will be loaded into memory. That is very confusing to the computer. Hence, there is the need for a new DLL file and a reboot.

Years ago, Microsoft initiated something called Patch Tuesday. On the second Tuesday of each month, Microsoft released security patches. Then they came out with Microsoft Update, in which the system checks for updates to other Microsoft products such as Microsoft Office. The most commonly used Office applications are Word, Excel, Access, PowerPoint, Publisher, and Outlook.

A computer in good running condition (no malware) shouldn't need to be rebooted except when required by software installation or updates.

Rebooting does not mean turning the computer off and on. For Windows, it means to click on the Start button, on the lower left corner of the screen, then click Turn Off Computer, then click Restart.

Rebooting a computer is the first-step remedy for most PC troubles. Rebooting returns all the computer's hardware and software to a known initial state. It's kind of like passing Go in Monopoly.

After the Start, Turn Off Computer, and Restart scenario, the next step is to disconnect all peripherals, such as printers, USB ports, speakers, and external drives. Then pull the plug on the computer. Wait 30 seconds. Next, plug the computer back into the wall socket or power strip. Hopefully, your computer problems are over.

Q70: *How do speakers work?*
· ·

A speaker uses the interaction of two magnetic fields to cause a paper or thin-metal diaphragm, called the cone, to vibrate back and forth. This produces sound, which is nothing more than the movement of air caused by something that vibrates.

The two parts of a sound wave are compression and rarefaction. Compression means that the air molecules are packed tightly together, and rarefaction means the air molecules are spread thinly. Sound is a series of compressions and rarefactions.

You can literally get a feel for sound by bringing the back of your hand close to your mouth as you talk. (Use your hand. You don't want to put your foot in your mouth.) The hairs on the back of the hand move back and forth according to the compressions and rarefactions of your voice.

A speaker cone must be able to move forward to produce a compression wave, i.e., to bunch up the air molecules. The cone must move back to produce a rarefaction wave.

A speaker has a permanent magnet with a north pole on one end and a south pole on the other end. A coil of fine wire, termed the voice coil, is placed close to one end of the permanent magnet. The coil is glued to the flexible speaker cone. Most speaker cones are made of paper.

Electric current from the amplifier is sent through the voice coil, making it an electromagnet. Electromagnets have a north pole and a south pole just like a permanent magnet. But which end is north and which end is south depend on which way the current goes through the coil. When one end of the electromagnet is a north pole, it pushes away from the north end of the permanent magnet. Remember that like poles repel and unlike poles attract. The cone moves forward and produces a compression wave that causes our eardrum to move inward.

When current is sent through in the opposite direction, the same end of the voice coil (electromagnet) becomes a south pole. The cone moves back and produces a rarefaction wave. This causes our eardrum to move outward.

So, the amplifier sends electric current to the speaker coil, which makes it an electromagnet that moves back and forth when its magnetic field repels or attracts the magnetic field of the permanent magnet.

Try this simple science experiment. Find an old speaker from a radio or television set. Touch the terminals of a battery to the terminals of the speaker. A small lantern battery, a 9-volt, D or C cell will all work.

Note which way the speaker cone moves when you just touch the terminals to the speaker. The cone will either move forward or backward. Now reverse the wires going to the speaker. Do you see the cone move in the opposite direction? You have produced a compression wave and a rarefaction wave.

Q71: If you tap into a telephone line, will you be able to listen to all the conversations being conducted?

Wiretapping is the monitoring of telephone and Internet conversations by a third party. Wiretapping seems to occur all the time in crime and spy movies. In reality, it is illegal in all developed democracies as a safeguard of a person's privacy. Wiretapping requires law enforcement agencies to get a court order.

We assume our phone lines are secure. And they probably are because nobody cares enough to listen. But if somebody wants to hear us order pizza or talk to Aunt Molly, it is quite easy.

Three bundled telephone wires come into your house. The conversation is carried on the red and green wires, and the ringer is the yellow wire. The receiver you pick up has a microphone you talk into, along with a speaker to put to your ear.

All you need for listening is the speaker part. If you wire or tap a handset across the red and green wire, you hear the conversation. These handsets are the same ones that linemen use to make sure your telephone is working. It is the same as adding another telephone to the telephones already in the house.

The tapper could splice into the line outside your house or at the junction box. He could attach a listening device or tape recorder that would activate whenever the phone is used. Such voice-activated recorders are often used for taking dictation by doctors, lawyers, CEOs, and writers.

Another method to tap a phone is to install a bug or tiny radio transmitter into the telephone receiver. Many of these bugs pick up any sound in the room, not just the telephone conversation. The receiver is placed in a nearby room, car, or van parked on the street. These listening devices are often depicted in movies. Keep in mind, however, that such activity is illegal.

Many of us use cordless phones. The handset has a radio transmitter that sends our conversations to a base unit. Anyone with a scanner can listen in on those conversations. However, the newer cordless phones that operate in the 1.9-, 2.4-, or 5.8-gigahertz range have a simple encryption technology that makes it harder for eavesdroppers to listen.

Are cell phones safe? Cell phones send radio signals to low-power transmitters located in "cells" that range in size from several hundred yards to 20 miles (32 kilometers) across. As you travel from cell to cell, the signal from your cell phone is transferred to the nearest transmitter/receiver tower. Most of the newer cell phone systems are digital, and more difficult for scanners to monitor.

What is the most threatening bit of "wiretapping" around? It's those hobbyists and corporate spies driving around the office or neighborhood using a laptop and free software that captures data transmitted to and from Wi-Fi computer networks and printers.

Here are some security precautions for you to consider. Use a wired-in telephone, not a cordless phone if you give credit card numbers and expiration dates when ordering stuff. Use a firewall and antivirus software on your computer. Use Web-based e-mail that has the secure https, not the normal http (notice the "s" on the end) if you order goods off the Internet. Never consider any e-mail to be confidential.

Q72: Why don't cell phones have a dial tone?

The dial tone is used to let the telephone user know that a signal is available and that the system is working. If no dial tone, no call can be placed.

Most cell phones have those little bars that inform the owner of the signal strength. If the cell phone is out of range of a cell tower, the cell phones usually display something like "network unavailable" or "no service" on the screen.

Keep in mind that even when you are not using your cell phone, it remains "on." The cell phone is a receiver, just like a radio receiver, but with the volume turned down. The cell phone is listening for any calls that might come in. A cell phone is "off" only when the power is turned off.

Early telephone systems all had a telephone operator, a real live person. In old Andy Griffin shows, Sheriff Andy Taylor would take the earpiece off the hook and say into the separate mouthpiece, "Sarah, get me Mr. Pilot." Then Deputy Barney Fife would say, "Sarah, ring me Juanita at the Bluebird Diner."

When telephone operations were automated, the automatic tone indicated the system was ready to be used. The British were the first to use a dial tone. The tone indicated that the telephone exchange was working, the receiver had been taken off the hook, and the telephone receiver was ready to talk into. The dial tone quit when the first number was dialed.

The United States started using dial tones in the late 1940s. Widespread use came in the 1950s. There is a story about President Dwight D. Eisenhower leaving the White House in 1961. He retired to his farm a tad south of Gettysburg, Pennsylvania. When he picked up his house phone, he didn't know what that strange noise was. One of his aides had to explain the dial tone to the former president, and also how to use a rotary phone.

Modern dial tones in the United States are a blend of two frequencies, tones, or pitches. One is 350 hertz and the other is 440 hertz. That 440 hertz dial tone has been used by stringed concert musicians to tune their instruments. In music, the A above middle C is written as A440.

Touch tone dialing, the current standard in the industry, started in 1963. Each number from 0 to 9, plus the star, pound, and A, B, C, and D buttons use two tones out of a possible eight. The lowest is 697 hertz and the highest is 1209 hertz. For example, when you hit the 6-button on the phone, it is a combination of 770 hertz and 1477 hertz that you hear.

Q73: *How do some eyeglasses turn dark in sunlight?*

L enses that darken in bright light are called photochromic lenses. The prefix *photo-*denotes "light," and the suffix *-chromic* designates a process producing change. Another common name is transition lenses. These lenses darken in response to ultraviolet light.

Crystals of silver chloride (AgCl) are embedded in the glass or plastic. When these crystals are exposed to UV light from the sun, the ionic compound AgCl is dissociated, or broken down, into silver atoms and chlorine atoms.

Those bunches of silver atoms provide the darkness of the glasses. Less light gets through and around the silver atoms.

When the transition lens wearer goes inside a building, away from the sun's ultraviolet rays, the silver and chlorine atoms combine again to form the ionic compound AgCl, and the lenses lighten.

The process is somewhat like the photographic process in which silver halide crystals are changed to silver to give a black-and-white image. In photography, the process is not reversible. The silver stays as silver and does not change back into silver halide.

One of the big advantages of photochromic lenses or transition lenses is that a user does not have to carry a separate pair of sunglasses. Not only do these lenses protect the eyes from a sun that is too bright, but they also block the harmful UV rays from the sun. UV rays can cause cataracts. Cataracts are cloudiness of the lens of the eye, which is normally clear. With cataracts, insufficient light reaches the retina of the eye. In severe cases, the lens may become opaque.

A disadvantage of photochromic lenses is that they do not change or transition immediately. There is a delay of one to three minutes for the glasses to darken. Auto drivers have also noticed that these photochromic lenses leave much to be desired. The windshield of a car blocks a lot of the UV light needed to darken the glasses.

The first ones were not that good. The darkening agent, silver chloride, was dispersed in the glass itself. The degree of darkening depended on the thickness of the glass, which varied according to the prescription. Manufacturers got around this problem by coating the material on the surface of a plastic lens. The coating is typically about .006 inch (150 micrometers) thick.

Q74: Why doesn't stainless steel rust?

Rusting occurs when metal reacts with oxygen in the air. Iron is especially vulnerable to rust, as the pure metal slowly changes into iron oxide, which is weak and crumbly. As the rust or oxidation reaction progresses, the surface area of the rusty part increases, and that speeds up the reaction. In addition, rust pushes on into the interior of the metal, ruining it.

Iron came in with the Iron Age, of course, and that was about 1800 BCE. After some time, people discovered that getting rid of the impurities in iron and mixing a bit of carbon produced a strong new metal called steel. Steel is very durable, but alas, it also will rust.

In the late 1800s, some smart people in Sheffield, England, were doing experiments on steel. They found that adding an element called chromium, about 13 percent, made the steel immune to rust. They called the new metal "stainless steel." It also oxidized, but in a weird sort of way.

Regular steel reacts with air to form a layer of iron oxide, a chemical word for rust. Stainless steel also reacts with air, but instead of iron oxide, the layer formed is chromium oxide. Once this layer forms, the oxidation stops. The so-called rust doesn't penetrate the metal and weaken it.

The chemists don't call it rusting. They use the term passivation. It is fast and effective. If a piece of stainless steel is scratched, a layer of chromium oxide will form over the scratch immediately. The "wound" is quickly healed.

There are other metals that do not rust easily. Aluminum won't rust unless it is bolted to another type of metal. Then a whole zoo of chemical reactions can take place to cause corrosion.

Titanium resists rust for decades. It is lightweight, has high strength, and can be alloyed or mixed with iron and aluminum to be used in jet engines, missiles, dental implants, jewelry, mobile phones, and numerous industrial and chemical processes.

If stainless steel is so good, why isn't all our steel stainless steel? Stainless steel is more expensive. Sometimes regular steel is stronger that stainless steel. Regular steel can be protected from rust by chemical treatment or by painting it.

One treatment is galvanization, whereby a layer of zinc is added to the surface of steel via a chemical reaction. You can buy galvanized nails, screws, bolts, nuts at a hardware store.

Take a look at the license plates on cars. If you spot a streak of red-brown rust extending downward from the two screws that attach the license plate to the car, you know the car owner used regular steel screws. More astute car owners will use stainless steel screws or those black zinc-plated screws.

Do you remember Ziebart? They applied an undercoating to cars and pickups to prevent rust formation. In 1990, Zeibart had more than 1,000 locations in 40 countries. Then car makers started using galvanized steel and applying an e-coating, which was an electronically applied primer. Modern cars simply don't rust out as badly or quickly as the old ones did.

Q75: What is safety glass?

S afety glass is most often associated with glass used in car windshields. Luckily, safety glass and the automobile came along at about the same time. In 1903, French chemist Édouard Benedictus knocked a glass flask off a shelf while climbing a ladder. The flask shattered when it hit the hard floor, but Benedictus noticed that the fragments of glass did not fly apart. Rather, the flask remained almost in its original shape.

Benedictus examined the flask and noticed that it had a film on the inside to which the broken pieces of glass adhered. This thin film or layer came from the evaporation of a solution of cellulose nitrate, which was prepared from cotton and nitric acid. The stuff inside had evaporated away, leaving a film on the inside of the flask.

Benedictus didn't do anything to follow up on his accidental discovery, except to attach a note or label to the flask. Some time later he heard about a young girl who had been badly cut by glass in a car accident in Paris. A few weeks later, he read in the newspaper about another serious injury from flying glass.

It suddenly occurred to him that his experience with the non-shattering glass flask offered a potential solution to the problem. Benedictus went to his lab, found that non-shattering glass flask and spent the next few days planning how a coating of some kind could be applied to make glass safe.

With the help of a letter press, he produced the first sheets of safety glass, referred to as "triplex." Each triplex consisted of a sandwich in which two sheets of glass had a sheet of cellulose nitrate between them. The three layers are bonded together with heat.

In 1909, Benedictus took out a patent on the new safety glass. Oddly, the first use of the newly invented safety glass was not in autos, but rather the lenses of gas masks in World War I. But then Henry Ford started using safety glass in 1919, and it became standard in windshields in all Ford cars by 1929.

You may have seen some of those early automobiles in which the windshields are yellowed with age. The cellulose nitrate layer between the sheets of glass turned yellow with exposure to sunlight, same as old newspapers.

By 1933, the cellulose nitrate was replaced with cellulose acetate, which was more resistant to coloration by sunlight, but lacked strength over a broad temperature range and produced haze. By 1940, a completely synthetic polymer, polyvinyl butyral (PVB) became the standard for laminated glass in cars and airplanes. PVB is a resin that has good bonding characteristics and excellent optical clarity. It is both tough and flexible.

Laminated safety glass is used in greenhouse windows, cutting boards, shower enclosures, office partitions, and glass doors in commercial buildings.

There is another type of safety glass that is not laminated, which means there is no sheet of plastic between layers of glass. It is known as tempered glass, and it shatters into many small pieces that are less harmful than larger shards of glass that can do major damage to a human.

This tempered glass is used in the side and rear windows of cars. Tempered glass is made by heating up the glass and then quickly cooling it. The tempering increases the strength of the glass. It breaks into little pebble-like pieces instead of shrapnel-like glass with very sharp edges.

Other typical uses of tempered glass are storm doors, doors in schools and hospitals and shopping centers, skylights, and computer monitors. You can see tempered safety glass in the rear windows of your car on a sunny day by wearing polarized sunglasses. As you move your head from side to side, you will notice a symmetrical pattern in the glass created during the tempering process.

Chapter Eight

At the Fringes of Science

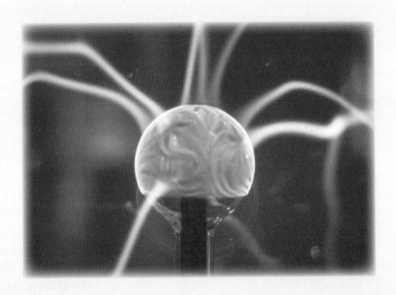

Q76: How did Atlantis fall?
· ·

One of the great mysteries of all time! Plato, the Greek father of Western philosophy, wrote about Atlantis in 360 BCE, almost 2,400 years ago. But his lost island continent of Atlantis was supposed to have been destroyed in 9000 BCE.

According to legend, Atlantis valued peace, wisdom, and art. The people of Atlantis had an advanced technological society. Their lands were rich, and they enjoyed abundant food, wood, animals, and flowers. Atlantis was a naval power that ruled much of the known earth at that time. But their leaders became greedy, corrupt, and started to invade their neighbors. Athens defeated the Atlantis military. Meanwhile, Atlantis lost the favor of the gods. Earthquakes, tsunamis, and floods swallowed up the island of Atlantis, and both it and its Athenian conquerors disappeared.

Plato's story is told using dialogue, a popular technique at the time. The three or four main speakers in the dialogue were all alive at the time of Plato. He was a master storyteller and employing the names of well-known people of his time lent credence to his work.

Locations various writers have suggested for Atlantis include the Greek islands and indeed anywhere around the Mediterranean Sea. The North Sea, the Canary Islands, Antarctica, the Caribbean, and anywhere in the Pacific have also been mentioned.

There are competing theories for the destruction of Atlantis, in addition to the earthquakes and floods described by Plato. A volcano could have erupted and buried Atlantis. An asteroid hit Atlantis. Aliens from outer space did it. Note: Anytime we can't explain something, those aliens always show up.

But there are problems with the Atlantis story. The earliest recorded history of any city was right around 8000 BCE. The city was a primitive little place in Turkey, and the people were hunter-gatherers. Tame cattle show up around 6000 BCE, and the first buildings appeared around 5000 BCE.

Some ancient writers claim Atlantis was real, while others say the story is Plato's warning against pride (hubris) and over-confidence. There is no proof that Atlantis ever existed. Modern scholars believe we should use the story of Atlantis to examine the ideas of government, power, greed, nationalism, and the relationships between countries.

Plato, who also wrote *The Republic*, lived to the age of 80. He was a student of Socrates, the grandfather of western philosophy. Aristotle was a student of Plato, and he went on to tutor Alexander the Great. Four famous Greeks in a row: Socrates, Plato, Aristotle, and Alexander (though he was Macedonian).

Q77: *Why do water droplets dance on a hot pan?*

The Leidenfrost effect is the phenomenon in which water in contact with a very hot surface is protected from evaporating away by a very thin vapor barrier. It was named after a German doctor and theologian, Johann Gottlob Leidenfrost, who wrote about the qualities of water in 1756.

Here's what happens. If you drop some water on a pan or skillet that is slightly below or above the boiling point of water, which is 212°F (100°C), the water will bead up and rather quickly evaporate away, much as expected.

Here's the odd part. If the temperature of the pan or skillet gets hotter, to about 400°F (204°C), one might expect the water to boil or evaporate away even more quickly. But it doesn't. Instead, the water will bead up into various size droplets and skitter around, lasting much longer than when the pan was at a lower temperature. At a really, really high temperature, way above that 400°F, the water droplets will disappear rather quickly due to evaporation.

So just how does this Leidenfrost effect work? The bottom of the drop, which is in contact with the hot pan, vaporizes. The water droplet then rides on a thin but protective vapor barrier. Some of those drops will dance around for as long as a minute or two.

There are three ways of conducting heat: conduction, convection, and radiation. Steam, vapor, or any gas is a very poor thermal conductor. So the heat from the pan or skillet cannot easily get through the vapor on which the drop is riding. That vapor layer is about one-tenth the thickness of a dime. The vapor acts as an insulator and keeps the droplet alive for quite some time. People who do a lot of cooking will notice the Leidenfrost effect.

The Leidenfrost effect was shown on the *MythBusters* show a few years back. A wet finger can be stuck into molten lead without any real danger, if precautions are taken. That is what they showed on their program. As soon as the wet finger touches the hot molten lead, the water on the finger turns to vapor and the finger is protected by that vapor barricade.

Some performers and instructors have walked on hot coals, which relies on the same phenomenon. Sweat or water on the bottom of the feet protects against some potentially bad burns.

Liquid nitrogen poured out on a floor exhibits the Leidenfrost effect. The drops and globs bead up as they skate across the floor. In this case, it is nitrogen vapor, not water vapor, that protects the drops for some time.

Q78: What are my chances of being killed in a car accident?

. . . .

They're pretty high, about 1 in 9,000 every year! This question brings up the fascinating topic of risk and how people perceive risk. Driving our cars is the single most dangerous activity we do on a regular basis. Perhaps it's because of all those who are driving drunk, or distracted by texting or talking on cell phones, or eating while driving, or spaced out on drugs, or speeding, or tired and falling asleep at the wheel.

Calculating risks is straightforward. Divide the number of people who ride in cars, which is nearly the population of the United States, around 300 million, by the number of people who are killed every year, about 33,000, and you come up with about 1 in 9,000 each year. It is about 1 in 80 over a lifetime. Over a lifetime, there is a 1 in 20 chance you and I will be in a car accident involving serious injury.

Air travel is far safer than driving in a car, but our view and feelings about the risks are skewed. A plane crash is terrifying to contemplate, having a high dread factor. Remember the middle of July 2014. In a little over one week, a Malaysia Airlines plane was shot down over the Ukraine, a Trans Asia plane crashed on landing off Taiwan, and an Air Algérie plane was lost in a dust storm in Mali. Three commercial plane accidents with a total loss of 462 passengers and crew, a tragedy that convinced many that they would never get on one of those things! During that same week, 735 people died in car crashes in the United States. Those car accident deaths make the local and statewide news, but do not garner the national spotlight.

The 9/11 attacks killed about 3,000 people, and we dutifully decry and mourn their loss. That same number, 3,000, are lost in car accidents every month in the United States. At times, we tend to go with our heart instead of our head. After the 9/11 terrorist attacks, many people decided to drive instead of fly. There was a spike in traffic deaths.

Cornell University did a study of the phenomenon and found that there were an additional 344 driving deaths per month in late 2001. The numbers decreased over time, of course, but the researchers attributed a total of 2,170 excess driving deaths due to the 9/11 attack. That is about 70 percent of the 3,000 directly killed in the attacks.

Sometimes our fears are not very rational. When those laser-scanning devices used to read the UPC label were put in checkout counters in supermarkets in the 1970s, the word *laser* was never used by storeowners and advertisers. Laser implied death rays, and who wants to die by getting zapped by a laser in the grocery store?

When nuclear magnetic resonance machines were introduced in 1977, people were reluctant to have anything to do with them and avoided them like the plague. They didn't want to be associated with anything nuclear. The profession changed the name to magnetic resonance imaging (MRI), and this new kind of X-ray machine caught on.

Risks in any human endeavor can be reduced, but never down to zero risk. You can decrease the risk of getting killed in a car accident by never getting into a car. But people have been killed when a car slams into the house or café. You can lessen your risk of getting killed in an airplane by not flying in an airliner. But aircraft have slammed into houses and killed people. Risks can't be minimized to zero.

We accept certain risks. There are more than 5,000 kids admitted to hospitals (very few deaths) every year when they swallow coins. We could make coins so large that kids couldn't put them in their mouth. But that destroys the utilitarian value of carrying coins in our pocket.

What are the top accident killers of people following traffic accidents? Falls are number two, with a 1-in-14,000 chance of dying. Fires are number three, with a 1-in-33,000 odds, and drowning is number 4 with 1-in-43,000 chance of departing this Earth.

When we get down to number 9, a lightning strike, with a 1-in-1,700,00 chance, people's perceptions are interesting. The victim is out fishing, or playing golf, or standing under a tree on a hill, or carrying an umbrella in a lightning and rainstorm. We don't think or say that they deserved to get struck by lightning, but the feeling is they should have been more prudent. The odds of getting killed by lightning is so small, we tend to put some culpability on the one that got struck.

Fortunately, most people don't dwell on thoughts of demise, death, and car accident fatalities. We just live our life, going about our activities and expecting nothing dreadful to occur.

Q79: How does time work?
. . . .

Time is a quantity and term that is very difficult to define. One dictionary says that time is "a period or interval," and another puts forth the definition as "a measurable interval." In his short story "The Time Professor," American author Ray Cummings wrote that "time is a method of preventing everything from happening at once." Nobel Prize–winning physicist Richard Feynman claimed that "time is just one damn thing after another."

Time is something that we can't see or sense, it just happens. Of course, for most of us we don't have enough of it and it goes by way too fast. And the older we get, the faster it goes! We realize we waste it foolishly and wish we had more of it.

We humans have found ways of measuring time. The day is the most obvious starting point, one rotation of the earth spinning on its axis. For most people, it is a period of daylight in which we work and a period of darkness or nighttime in which we sleep. Our bodies are tuned to this natural clock.

The year is also a measure of time: one revolution, or orbit, of the earth around the sun. This is approximately 365.25 days. That extra quarter of a day is why we have leap year every four years.

The origin of the month is one revolution, or orbit, of the moon around the earth. But because our calendar doesn't stick exactly to the moon's schedule, some of our months have more days than other months. So months get complicated, such as sidereal, synodic, and tropical months, but your basic month is based on the moon.

We use clocks to divide the day into smaller increments and we employ calendars to group days into larger increments. Both the dividing into smaller and grouping into larger have a long and fascinating history going way back to 900 BCE when the Egyptians made a sundial with a base that marked off a scale with six divisions. There is speculation that we get our 60 minutes in an hour and 60 seconds in a minute from the Egyptian sundial, but no one knows for sure.

Those Egyptians also had a calendar with 12 months of 30 days each, giving them 360 days in a year. That division is also why we have 360 degrees in a circle.

We do know that the Romans gave us the a.m. (ante meridiem) and p.m. (post meridiem). A clerk to the Roman consul had the job of noticing when the sun crossed the meridian, which is directly overhead. He had to announce it in the Forum, because lawyers had to appear in court before noon.

Daylight Saving Time was first proposed by Benjamin Franklin but actually came into use during World War I. The Germans were the first to adopt it, then Great Britain, followed by the United States. It was an attempt to adjust daylight hours in the summer to more closely match the hours that people are awake. The goal was to save fuel by lowering the need for artificial light.

Not everyone on Earth can have the sun directly overhead at the same time. So time zones were established, dividing the earth into 24 zones of 15 degrees each. Everyone in the same time zone sets their clock to the same time. You will recognize that 24 multiplied by 15 gives 360, the number of degrees in one rotation or circle. Each time zone is one hour different from the next.

The United States is spread across six different time zones: Eastern, Central, Mountain, Pacific, Alaska, and Hawaii. When it is 4 p.m. in New York, it is 3 p.m. in Tomah, Wisconsin, 2 p.m. in Denver, 1 p.m. in Los Angeles, noon in Juneau, Alaska, and 10 a.m. in Honolulu, Hawaii.

All time zones are measured from the Greenwich Observatory in England. An imaginary line running from the north pole, through Greenwich, to the south pole is referred to as the prime meridian. The international date line is on the opposite side of Earth, 180 degrees from the prime meridian. When you cross the international date line from west to east, you subtract a day, and if you cross the line from east to west, you add a day.

A pico second is one trillionth of a second and is the shortest period of time that can be measured. A millisecond is a thousandth of a second and is roughly the length of time the shutter is open on a camera to take a picture without human motion causing a blur. A second is the average time for a human heartbeat. Forty days is the longest a person can survive without food. Recorded history goes back around 5,000 years. Planet Earth comes in at about 4.5 billion years old, and the universe is dated to be about 13.8 billion years.

Q80: *Why do my hands get warmer when I rub them together?*
. . . .

F riction happens when any two objects rub against each other. Friction is a force that opposes the direction of motion. If you just put your hands together, there is no opposition or resistance to motion. Rub them together and you have friction. When we do work to overcome friction, some of that energy goes into heat.

The irregularities on the surfaces act as obstructions to motion. Even objects that appear perfectly smooth, such as sheets of glass, have irregular surfaces if viewed under a microscope.

Friction can occur between two solid objects, such as your hands. But friction can also occur between a liquid and a solid. An example would be a ship being slowed by water. Friction can even happen between a solid and a gas, like a car being slowed by air resistance.

The degree or amount of friction depends on the roughness or smoothness of the two surfaces and the amount of pressure applied to the objects. Gravity pulls down on everything, and objects with more mass have more friction and are more difficult to move. Pulling a big chunk of iron across a floor is more difficult than pulling the same size block of wood across the floor. That assumes, of course, that both have the same degree of smoothness or roughness.

As a general rule, two solid objects have more friction than two liquid objects, or a solid one and a liquid one. This is why we might slip on a wet sidewalk, but not on a dry one.

Sometimes we want maximum friction. We desire a good amount of friction between our car tires and the road surface, since otherwise the car would slide on a wet or icy road or when going around a curve. We want good friction between our shoes and the floor or sidewalk.

At other times, we try to reduce friction, such as when we wax skis to reduce friction and drag, or use ice skates on the rink. The small amount of friction between the skate blade and ice melts the ice, so the ice skater is actually water skiing! If we use soap on our hands and rub them together, the friction just about disappears. Layers of smooth molecules permit the hands to glide pass each other, reducing the resistance between them.

We spend a good deal of effort and money to reduce friction when metal rubs against metal, both to reduce friction and to lessen heat buildup. Lubricants in our cars and trucks prevent engine-damaging heat. Parts would break down real fast without oil to reduce the friction.

Friction seems like a straightforward concept. But oddly enough, friction is not well understood at the molecular level. Scientists do know that when two objects rub together, the rough edges on one object sort of snag on the rough edges of the other object. The atoms cling together at many points of contact. Some of the objects' energy has to be used to break off those rough edges so that the objects can keep moving. As the sliding continues, the atoms snap apart or are torn from one surface by the other.

It's that tearing off of molecules that we witness when an object is being worn down, such as the thinning soles of our shoes and rubber wearing off on our car tires.

Technically, there exist both static friction and sliding friction. Static friction occurs when an object is not moving, and sliding friction happens when an object is moving. Picture a wood block sitting atop a length of board. We slowly raise one end of the board. The block remains in place on the board. Static friction, the friction between the board and the block, prevents the wood block from moving. Continue raising the end of the board, and there comes a point where the wood block starts sliding down the board. There is now sliding friction between the wood block and the board. As a general rule, static friction is greater than sliding friction.

We note the difference between static friction and sliding friction in braking a car in an emergency. If we jam on the brakes when we see that deer in front of us, the wheels lock in place. When wheels lock, the tires slide, providing less friction than if they are made a rotate to a stop. When a tire is rolling. its surface does not slide along the road. The friction applied by the rolling tires is static friction, and it is greater than sliding friction.

Many many years ago, we were taught to pump the brakes when we need to stop suddenly. But that's not what we normal people do in a panic situation, such as when we're looking at a road map and the vehicle in front of us has suddenly stopped. We jam on the brakes.

Auto manufacturers have figured out what we mortals actually do, so they introduced the anti-lock braking system (ABS) in the 1970s and it is standard on most cars today. ABS automatically pumps the brakes, locking and unlocking the brakes, while our foot remains firmly planted on the brake pedal. The driver can then concentrate on steering safely.

Q81: Where does the light go when you turn off the light switch?

Turn a light switch on and the room fills with light. Flip the switch off and the light disappears. But where does it disappear to?

Clearly, no light can simply disappear. The most sacred law of science, the law of conservation of energy, says so. Matter and energy cannot be created or destroyed. Matter and energy can only change from one form to another.

When the lightbulb is turned on, electrons go through a filament. The filament in a lightbulb is typically made of tungsten, which presents some resistance to electron flow. As a result, the filament gets so hot it emits light, tiny particles or waves called photons.

These pieces of light bounce around at a speed of 186,000 miles (300,000 kilometers) per second, hitting things and bouncing off them. Some of the light is absorbed and some is reflected.

The things that light hits, such as the walls and curtains and the cat, are made up of atoms. Consider these atoms to be like tiny billiard balls or perhaps marbles. When light hits these atoms, it transfers its energy. The atom gets a bit of a jolt, which causes it to vibrate.

The vibrating atom jostles against its neighbor atoms and causes them to vibrate a bit. A ripple effect occurs. It's much like a rock thrown into a smooth pond. The kinetic energy of the rock spreads to atoms in the water and moves out to more and more water molecules, causing a wave.

The ripple effect of a rock in water is easy for us humans to see. Light hitting atoms in the room is a bit subtler, but it's the same idea. The vibrating atoms cause a slight temperature rise. The wall is just a bit warmer than before the light hit it. The light is absorbed as thermal energy.

Carry this to extremes by moving your hand closer to the lightbulb. You can feel the heat. Even a conventional flashlight will be sufficient to warm the back of your hand. Sunlight hitting your face is a more extreme case. Direct sunlight is far stronger than a lightbulb or flashlight.

So some light in a room is absorbed by the walls, and some is reflected, allowing us to see the walls. Flip the switch off and no more light enters the room. But why doesn't what's already there keep reflecting as it bounces back and forth between the walls? Well, the light travels extremely fast (at the speed of light). It bounces off so many walls, being partially absorbed with each bounce, that before our hand has left the switch, all the light has been absorbed. It's dark in the room, and we trip over the cat on our way out the door.

Fluorescent bulbs produce light differently than incandescent lamps. An electric current stimulates mercury vapor that produces ultraviolet light. The invisible ultraviolet light causes a phosphor coating on the inside of the lamp to glow. A compact fluorescent lamp (CFL) generates light by the same method as those long fluorescent tubes.

The relatively new lighting kid on the block is a light emitting diode (LED). No filament to get hot, no mercury vapor, no ultraviolet light striking phosphors, no vacuum in a bulb. Illumination comes about by movement of electrons in a semiconductor material. LED lighting is a clever manipulation of elements such as silicon, germanium, carbon, aluminum, arsenic, and others. LEDs stay cool, seemingly last forever, and are extremely energy efficient. LEDs are the unsung heroes in the electronics world of computers, displays, televisions, and all sorts of indicator lights.

Q82: What are some science predictions that did not come true?

There have been some real blunders and bloopers in the past 100 years or more. Lord Kelvin was the president of the Royal Society in England and considered one the greatest scientists of all time. He made landmark discoveries in the study of heat and electricity in the years just prior to 1900. Lord Kelvin said that heavier-than-air flying machines were impossible. He also declared that "X-rays will prove to be a hoax and radio has no future." Today, airplanes, X-rays, and radio are routinely used in everyday life.

Dr. Lee de Forest was the inventor of the vacuum tube and the father of television. He was awarded more than 180 patents. Dr. de Forest was adamant about space travel. "Man will never reach the moon regardless of all future scientific advances," he claimed. On live television, more than 600 million people worldwide watched Neil Armstrong step onto the moon in July 1969.

"The bomb will never go off. I speak as an expert in explosives," stated Admiral William Leahy, when asked about the atomic bomb being developed in Los Alamos. Admiral Leahy was the chief of staff to Presidents Franklin D. Roosevelt and Harry S. Truman. The atomic bomb "went off" over Hiroshima and Nagasaki on August 6 and August 9, 1945. The Japanese surrendered on September 2, 1945, saving thousands of lives on both sides.

Thomas Watson, chairman of IBM, declared in 1943, "I think there is a world market for maybe five computers." Watson was a self-made industrial leader and was said to the world's greatest salesman. He was one of the richest men in the world when he passed away in 1956. Most estimates place the number of computers in 2017 to be about 2 billion worldwide.

Who could argue with Albert Einstein? But Einstein was not right about everything. "There is not the slightest indication that nuclear energy will ever be obtainable. It would mean that the atom would have to be shattered at will," Einstein postulated in 1932. As of 2017, there are 99 nuclear reactors in 30 of our United States, producing 20 percent of our electrical needs. Worldwide there are 439 reactors and 67 under construction. Nuclear energy is widely employed in medicine, propulsion, food preservation, smoke detectors, materials processing, and a myriad of other processes.

"The earth's crust does not move," was a generally accepted geological precept up to the early 1900s. In 1912, the meteorologist Alfred Wegener described what he called continental drift, expanded in his 1915 book, *The Origin of Continents and Oceans.* Some 50 years later, we know the phenomena as plate tectonics. The earth's outer shell (lithosphere) consists of a half dozen major plates and numerous smaller ones. The plates are continually on the move.

Dr. Peter Duesberg, molecular-biology professor at UC Berkeley, said in 1988, "That virus is a pussycat." He was talking about HIV, the virus that causes AIDS. When a person is infected with HIV, the virus attacks and weakens the immune system. Best estimates are that 40 million people have died of AIDS worldwide from that "pussycat" virus.

At one time, most people thought that stomach ulcers were caused by stress, spicy food, and too much acid. That belief was also generally accepted by the medical profession. Australian physiologist Dr. Barry James Marshall, proved that the *Helicobacter pylori* bacteria caused gastric inflammation.

In 1985, Dr. Marshall deliberately infected himself with the bacterium to prove that *H. pylori* causes gastritis and peptic ulcers. In 2005, Dr. Marshall and his collaborator, J. Robin Warren, were awarded the Nobel Prize in Physiology or Medicine.

Q83: Why is seeing a black cat or walking under a ladder considered unlucky?

. . . .

In ancient Egypt, black cats were revered. Today, Americans keep 81 million cats as pets, and some of them are black.

One misplaced belief is that a black cat crossing in front of you is bad luck. The old superstition arises from the suggestion that witches may take the form of domestic animals.

Not walking under a ladder may be a very practical superstition. A ladder may indicate that somebody is up above you, maybe on top of the ladder or on a roof. The person just might drop something and conk you on the head. Why take a chance? Still, the origins of this worry may be illogical. One hypothesis suggests that a ladder resembles a medieval gallows. Another comes from the Christian belief in the Holy Trinity. A stepladder or ladder leaning against a wall forms a triangle, and messing with that triangle would be blasphemy.

Cats and ladders are just two of a whole menu of irrational fears and phobias. How about breaking a mirror? That dooms you to seven years of bad luck, so goes the thinking of some. This superstition is said to arise from the belief that mirrors don't just reflect your image, but that they hold pieces of your soul.

Three sixes in a row can strike fear in the hearts of the timid. In the Book of Revelations, 666 is the number of the "beast" and is thought by some to be the sign of Satan. Many folks interpret 666 as a sign of the end of time. Does any of you have a string of 666 in your phone number, license plate, Social Security number, or zip code?

The number 13 has a long history of being an unlucky number. Can you believe that some hotels do not have a 13th floor and some airplanes skip the 13th row? Fear of Friday the 13th is a widespread phobia and has its own term, *triskaidekaphobia*, which is an extreme suspicion of the number 13. But if a hotel does not have a 13th floor, isn't floor 14 really the 13th floor?

Cornell psychologist Dr. Thomas Gilovich explained it best. "If something bad happens to you on Friday the thirteenth, the two will be forever associated in your mind. All those Friday the thirteenth days with no extraordinary occurrences will be forgotten and ignored."

A rabbit's foot is lucky and will deflect any evil, so the belief goes. Good-luck rabbit's feet go back to the time of the Celtic tribes in Britain around 600 BCE.

All of us have some fears and phobias, and yes, probably hold to a superstition or two. Some fear public speaking. Others have an aversion to needles, or enclosed spaces, or heights. Others are afraid of animals such as bats and snakes. Some, like football coach and commentator John Madden, have a pathologic fear of flying. A bus carried him from game to game.

Baseball players are quite prone to superstitions. Watch carefully and you'll see some pitchers avoid stepping on the first- or third-base line when walking to or from the mound. Chipper Jones, who spent his entire 19-year Major League career with the Atlanta Braves, entered into the Hall of Fame in 2018, his first year of eligibility. He played computer solitaire right up to game time every night. Andy Pettitte won five league championships with his New York Yankees. He would listen to the entire *Rocky* soundtrack on the day he pitched. Wade Boggs ate only chicken before a game. Tim Lincecum wore the same hat every time he was pitching for the San Francisco Giants.

Chapter Nine

Science Mystery and History

Q84: *Why does toast land jelly-side down?*
. . . .

I grew up on a farm outside of Seneca in rural Crawford County in southwest Wisconsin. I was fortunate be a part of the greatest educational system ever devised in our country—a one-room country school. No indoor plumbing, no indoor toilets, and no telephone. But we had one excellent teacher with 28 kids in grades one through eight in a school no bigger than a garage.

After walking home, we changed into working clothes and went out to "do the chores." We would spread some homemade jelly on homemade bread before heading out to the barns, sheds, and fields.

More than once, I dropped my jellied slice of bread on the ground, and if memory serves me right, it always seemed to land jelly-side down. Now, jelly-side up would be OK, just brush it off and go out to the meet the cows. But jelly-side down is a ruined snack.

We tested this theory when I was teaching rotation in my high school physics class. We gently slid a piece of wood off a smooth horizontal surface at various heights. The wood was the same size and shape as a slice of bread.

The results of our research showed that if the toast had a fall of 18 inches (46 centimeters), it made a half turn and always landed jelly-side down. If the toast fell about 42 inches (107 centimeters), it made one full rotation and always landed jelly-side up.

At intermediate heights, the toast landed on its edge and flipped one way or the other, with no predictability. Of course, if the fall height was closer to 18 inches, there was a greater chance of jelly-side down, and if closer to 42 inches, there was a better chance of jelly-side up. As a kid I had no idea that there was any scientific basis to which way my jelly-covered bread landed.

One of the joys of life is learning about cause and effect, learning about new things, and finding answers to imponderables.

Q85: Why does urine smell bad after eating asparagus?
. . . .

B lame it on asparagusic acid. When the body digests asparagus, enzymes break the vegetable down into sulfur compounds. The process takes place within 15 to 30 minutes of ingesting. Any compound with the word *sulfur* implies something offensive to the nose. Other sulfur-bearing substances include skunk spray, garlic, onions, and rotten eggs.

The asparagus phenomenon is not new. John Arbuthnot wrote in 1731 that "asparagus affects the urine with a foetid (fetid) smell." Marcel Proust added that "the vegetable transforms my chamber pot into a flask of perfume." In 1781, Benjamin Franklin penned, "A few Stems of Asparagus eaten shall give our Urine a disagreeable odour (odor)." Franklin was urging research by the Royal Academy of Brussels "to discover some Drug that shall render the natural Discharges of Wind from our Bodies, not only inoffensive, but agreeable as Perfumes."

Studies from the 1980s found that some people do not have the metabolic ability to create asparagus urine. They do not produce those volatile odoriferous compounds. An equally large number of people do not detect abnormal-smelling urine. The problem is rooted not only in production of the stench, but also in the detection of the aroma. Definitive studies done in 2010 found that nearly all people produce the foul sulfur compounds. A single genetic mutation, a switched base pair in a cluster of 50 different genes that do the coding for nose receptors, seems to be the culprit for those who cannot detect the smell.

There is one material to which manufacturers add a sulfur-based chemical. Natural gas has no odor of its own. The pungent rotten-egg smell of natural gas is caused by the gas company adding methyl mercaptan or thiophane. It is a safety measure so that we can detect any natural gas leak.

An unsavory odor in the urine is nothing to be alarmed over. Asparagus is available year-round, but spring is the best season for this nutritious vegetable. Crops are harvested from late February to June, with April being the prime month and high season for asparagus. A person might want to just go ahead and enjoy the succulent shoots.

Q86: Why do we see so many pieces of truck tires lying on the Interstate?

Studies by the National Highway Traffic Safety Administration indicate that road hazards are the leading cause of tire failure. The tires simply hit something on the roadway, accounting for 38 percent of tire losses. Other causes are improper inflation, improper mounting of the tires on the rims, and manufacturing defects.

Some tires that fail are retreads. New rubber is bonded to an old bald tire. Anytime you swing something around, it wants to go to the outside. If a truck is going 50 miles (81 kilometers) per hour and the retread rubber weighs 20 pounds (9 kilograms), there is more than 2,000 pounds (900 kilograms) of force that tries to pull the retreaded rubber off the old tire casing. That is 100 times what it weighs!! (There is a neat way to calculate the force. The centripetal acceleration is velocity squared divided by the radius.) The bonding between old tire and new rubber often is broken. If the truck is going 70 miles (110 kilometers) per hour, the force that wants to pull the retreaded rubber off is more than 4,000 pounds (1,800 kilograms), or 2 tons.

Retread is the term used to mean adding additional new material to extend the life of the tire. Recap means the tread is replaced, but not the sidewall. In one process, hot cure or mold cure, the tire is covered with uncured rubber and then cured in a mold the same as making a new tire.

In the cold cure process a pre-cured thread ring is applied to the tire casing. Both are put in a rubber envelope under vacuum and cured in a heating chamber. Curing means that the rubber is treated with a chemical to improve its hardness, strength, and elasticity.

Although at first glance it seems that retread tires would come apart more easily than new tires, studies show that the incidences of tire failure in new and retread tires are almost identical. One factor is common in both types of tire failure: overheating. Thirty percent of tires found on the highway show signs of overheating. Often a rotating tire will become deflated, overheat, and after several miles, start to shred.

Q87: How, why, and where did the Space Shuttle Challenger go down in 1986?

The Space Shuttle Challenger broke up on Tuesday, January 28, 1986 at 10:38 a.m. CST. Launched from Kennedy Spacecraft Center, the 25th shuttle mission, a vehicle with seven astronauts aboard, disintegrated 73 seconds into launch. It was about 9 miles (15 kilometers) high and going about 1,500 miles (2,400 kilometers) per hour. Because it was moving so fast, the crew compartment traveled up another 3 miles (5 kilometers) before it reached its peak altitude of about 12 miles (19 kilometers).

All shuttle flights are launched toward the east out over the Atlantic Ocean. The rotation of the earth from west to east imparts a speed of close to 1,000 miles (1,600 kilometers) per hour in the direction the shuttle is going. It's like a free "kick in the pants." The speed needed to get into orbit around the earth is 17,500 miles (28,200 kilometers) per hour, which works out to about 5 miles (8 kilometers) per second.

What was the cause of the accident? The shuttle is powered by three main engines that are fed liquid hydrogen and liquid oxygen, both stored in a large external tank (ET). The shuttle is also powered by two solid rocket boosters (SRBs), one on each side of and strapped to the ET. The fuel is ammonium perchlorate and aluminum. It is poured into the casting, much like pouring fudge candy. It hardens and feels like a pencil eraser.

The SRBs are about 150 feet (45.7 meters) long and made in four segments, designed so each segment fits on a railroad car and can be railed back to Utah for refilling.

The shuttle was destroyed after the lowest joint on the right hand SRB failed. The two O rings allowed a breach or opening for extremely hot gases from inside the rocket engine to hit the SRB attachment hardware, then the ET.

Two events happened at about the same time. The hydrogen tank, the lower part of the ET, ruptured due to the hot gases burning through the tank, and the SRB pivoted into the top of the ET. It was aerodynamic forces that tore the shuttle apart, not the big explosive fireball we see on TV and in pictures. The fireball was a result of the disintegration of the shuttle system and the igniting of the volatile fuels. Both SRBs survived the breakup of the shuttle system, and were seen increasing in altitude and gyrating on erratic paths. The SRBs were remotely destroyed by the range safety officer before they could come back over land and do damage.

A cold weather system had moved through Florida the night before the launch. The cold temperatures made the O rings brittle and unable to seal properly. Even so, the shuttle might have made it through the 130 seconds needed for the SRBs to burn, except for the shear winds at altitude that buffeted the vehicle.

Investigation and analysis after the accident indicated that when Challenger broke apart, the crew compartment remained intact. Several of the emergency oxygen packs had been manually turned on. Investigations after the accident showed that the oxygen remaining in the tanks was consistent with the expected usage during the 105-second fall to the ocean.

But the seven astronauts could not have survived the impact with the ocean, hitting the water at more than 200 miles (320 kilometers) per hour. The crew compartment was found six weeks after the accident in several hundred feet of water and roughly 20 miles (32.2 kilometers) east off the Florida coast. The bodies of all seven crewmembers were found strapped in their seats. They were returned to their families.

Commander Francis Scobee and pilot Michael Smith were buried in Arlington National Cemetery, mission specialist Ronald McNair in Lake City, South Carolina, and mission specialist Ellison Onizuka in the National Cemetery in Hawaii. Payload specialist Gregory Jarvis and mission specialist Judith Resnick were cremated, and their ashes scattered over the ocean.

Teacher and mission specialist Christa McAuliffe was interned in Concord, New Hampshire, not far from the classroom in which she taught.

Q88: Did bad weather cause the disappearance of Amelia Earhart?

Amelia Earhart, her navigator Fred Noonan, and her Lockheed Model 10 twin engine Electra airplane disappeared over the Pacific Ocean on July 2, 1937.

Prior to her round-the-world flight, Earhart had established a reputation as a woman aviator by being the first to fly the Atlantic Ocean in 1928, only one year after Charles Lindbergh's transatlantic New York to Paris flight. She was accompanied by a pilot friend.

She was the first woman to fly solo across the North American continent and back, making the trip in August 1928. In 1932, Amelia Earhart was the first woman to fly solo across the Atlantic Ocean, flying from Newfoundland and forced down in a cow pasture in Ireland. She encountered icing conditions and mechanical problems with the plane.

Earhart was awarded the Distinguished Flying Cross. She flew First Lady Eleanor Roosevelt over New York City. In 1935, she became the first person to fly solo from Honolulu, Hawaii, to Oakland, California. Earhart did long-distance air racing, set seven women's speed and distance records, and joined Purdue University's staff as a visiting professor.

Amelia Earhart and Eleanor Roosevelt were frequently tied in polls as the most admired women in 1930s America. Earhart had her own line of clothing and luggage. She wrote for *McCall's* magazine and hawked Lucky Strike cigarettes.

Extensive planning and fund-raising went into Earhart's 1937 around-the-world flight. Final plans called for a west-to-east trip, starting with great fanfare on June 1, 1937 from Miami, Florida. On June 29, Earhart and her navigator, Fred Noonan, reached Lae, New Guinea.

Their final three hops were to be from Lae, New Guinea, to Howland Island, then Howland Island to Hawaii, and finally Hawaii back to Oakland. Howland Island is a small strip of land a bit over a mile long, a third of a mile wide, (.6 square miles or 1.6 square kilometers), and 15 feet (4.6 meters) above Pacific Ocean level.

Amelia Earhart and Fred Noonan left Lae, New Guinea, heading east on July 2, 1937. They were never seen again.

To answer the question directly, the weather was not a factor, except perhaps a stronger headwind than expected. A whole series of misunderstandings, poor planning, and plain bad luck are blamed for the loss of the plane and crew.

There was confusion about which radio frequencies to use between Earhart's plane and a USCGS *Itasca*. The aircraft tanks were not completely full on take-off. Earhart was not that familiar with the new radios installed for the trip. There is evidence that a direction-finding antenna on Earhart's Lockheed Electra aircraft was torn off on the take-off from Lae. The crew didn't think they would need it. But the charts Noonan relied on had Howland Island 5 miles (8 kilometers) off target.

The last known transmission from Earhart was at 8:43 a.m. It was reported by the USCGS *Itasca* to be very strong, so they were very close to Howland Island. But nothing more was heard. After two weeks of a massive search effort by 9 ships and 66 aircraft, no evidence of the plane or its two crew members was ever found. Despite many conspiracy theories and speculations, most investigators believe they simply ran out of fuel and ditched at sea.

The Superior Court of Los Angeles declared Amelia Earhart legally dead two years after she and Noonan disappeared. The International Group for Historic Aircraft Recovery (TIGHAR) searched the area with sonar in June 2013. They got "some interesting images," but nothing definitive.

Q89: Why are the letters on a typewriter or keyboard mixed up?

The first typewriters were made in the mid 1870s by the Remington Company. Mark Twain was one of the first writers to use one. The standard keyboard (QWERTY) was designed by Christopher Latham Sholes in 1872. Sholes sold his interest to Remington, the same company that later made rifles.

Typewriters use a mechanism in which the alphabet letters are set into the end of a long bar. When a key is struck, the linkage swings the lettered bar into contact with a tape coated with ink. The ink is transferred to paper positioned right behind the tape.

Sholes arranged the keys so that the most commonly used letters were on opposite sides of the keyboard. This array tended to cause less jamming. The most common letters were placed where the nimblest fingers, the second and third, could reach them easily.

Typewriters have gone the way of the horse and buggy. Schools now have keyboarding classes instead of typing classes. Computer keyboards are laid out much like typewriters, but with a lot more function keys. The US keyboard on computers is pretty much the standard for the world. Ireland and the United Kingdom have some very slight differences. In Germany, as well as much of Central Europe, the Y and Z are swapped. In France, the A and Q are swapped as well as the Z and W.

Most European keyboards have the € symbol for the Euro. Some newer keyboards in the United States have the Euro (€) symbol, but older models do not. If you want to look at the symbol, hold down Alt while typing the numbers 0128 on the numeric keypad of a PC computer. When you let up on the Alt key, the Euro (€) symbol appears on your screen.

Christopher Sholes, inventor of the QWERTY keyboard, moved from Pennsylvania to Milwaukee as a teen, became a newspaper publisher, served in the Wisconsin Senate and Assembly, and campaigned successfully to abolish capital punishment in Wisconsin. Sholes died of tuberculosis in 1890. His daughter Lillian became known as the world's first typist. She worked in her father's office. Those first machines only did capital letters.

The "fastest typist in the world" title goes to Barbara Blackburn of Salem, Oregon, who was clocked in 2005 at 150 words per minute for 50 minutes. Her top speed was 212 wpm.

Q90: Why does grease make white paper transparent?
. . . .

The answer has to do with light and how it interacts with matter. Light can be absorbed, reflected, refracted, scattered, and dispersed.

Absorbed means the light hits something and doesn't bounce off. Reflection is quite straightforward. Light hits something and bounces off at the same angle it hit. Mirrors make use of reflection. Refraction is the bending of light. For example, light bends when it passes from air to water. Objects underwater appear to be in a different position. (That's something that spear-fishing people know something about.) Scattering refers to bouncing off or reflecting in many different directions. Dispersion means that light is broken up into seven colors.

When light hits a piece of paper, some is scattered in every direction, some is reflected back to the eye, and some is absorbed. The amount of each depends on the kinds of fibers that make up the paper and all the little air spaces between the fibers. Light must pass from air to paper and back and forth many times, all the while getting bent and scattered. Because all wavelengths of light are reflected and scattered equally, the paper appears white. The same kind of thing happens when light hits snow, or white cotton candy, or a Q-tip.

When soaked or coated with oil, grease, butter, or fat, the paper has all the tiny air spaces filled in. Light doesn't have to do all that bouncing and scattering. It only must pass from air through the grease. Light does not have to pass from paper back to the eye. The paper is transparent, or to be more technically correct, translucent. We can read words right through the paper.

The amount that light is refracted is called the index of refraction. Diamond has an index of refraction of 2.42. Glass has an index of refraction of about 1.5. Water has an index of refraction of 1.33. Simply put, glass bends light more than water, and diamond bends light more than glass.

The oil, grease, or fat has about the same index of refraction as paper. So the amount of scattering is kept to a minimum. Most of the light that would be scattered from the not-oiled paper is now transmitted through the paper.

Think back to snow. Snow and ice are both made of water. Snow has all those particles with air trapped in between them. A whole bunch of reflecting, refracting, and scattering is going on. We can't see through snow, same as paper. Ice does not have all those little facets and pockets of air, so the light goes right through, same as greased paper. It really is quite miraculous!

Let us turn our eyes from paper to the heavens. A rainbow, most people would agree, is one of nature's most beautiful and exquisite sights. Sir Isaac Newton was the one who worked out the angles of how light interacts with a raindrop. Light is refracted (bent) as it enters the raindrop. Some is reflected off the far side and refracted again as it leaves the raindrop and shoots down to the observer. Each time light is refracted it is also dispersed, with the shorter blue light waves bent more than the longer red. That is why the raindrop can take in a ray of light and give us an array of color.

Q91: Are viruses alive or dead?

· ·

Viruses inhabit a strange world at the boundary of living and non-living things. Viruses have been described as "organisms at the edge of life." Living things have certain characteristics such as being active and able to grow, reproduce, respond to stimuli, evolve, and consume energy.

If an organism is alive, it should be able to reproduce itself. Viruses do reproduce, but in a rather devious and underhanded way. They can multiply themselves only by infecting living cells, called host cells, and taking over the cell's chemical machinery so that they can make copies of themselves.

Outside of living cells, viruses show no signs of life. They cannot harness energy by themselves. They cannot react to the world around them or reproduce without pulling off the hijacking caper. Viruses are so small they weren't seen until 1931 with the invention of the electron microscope by two German engineers.

Viruses are tiny amounts of genetic material inside a casing made of protein. A virus is so devious, and the chemical structure so precise, that dried viruses can form crystals. If the crystals are dissolved in water, the virus can come "alive" and infect a host.

Viruses quite often get in the news: avian flu, West Nile virus, HIV, and Ebola. There are viruses we've known about for decades: the common cold, foot and mouth disease, hepatitis, mumps, rubella, yellow fever, chickenpox, smallpox, measles, rabies, and polio.

A virus attaches to a host cell. The virus enters or releases its genetic instructions into the host cell. The virus gives instructions to the host cell's enzymes, which then make parts for more virus particles. The new parts assemble into new viruses. These new virus particles leave the host cell, ready to infect other cells. It is just so cunning!

Fortunately, our body has a defense—our immune system. The system is complex, being made up of different types of cells, tissues, and enzymes. White blood cells patrol our body, looking for an antigen. An antigen is any foreign substance such as a chemical, bacteria, pollen, or virus. White blood cells signal the body to produce an antibody to go fight against the antigen.

Sometimes the body can use some help. That's where vaccines come to the rescue. Vaccines are made of the same material that makes us sick but are weak or attenuated. The measles, mumps, and rubella (MMR) vaccine is an example. The vaccines train the body to defend against viruses that invade it. The immune system learns to recognize and attack infections when exposed later in life. A person may not get sick at all or have a mild case.

Smallpox threatened George Washington's Continental Army. He himself had been slightly scarred as a young man by the dread disease. In February 1777, while encamped at Morristown, New Jersey, Washington wrote to Patrick Henry that smallpox "is more destructive to an Army in the Natural way, than the Enemy's Sword." Years before, smallpox had struck Britain's Northern Army at Quebec, making thousands unfit for duty. One in three died, and recruiting suffered.

Inoculation was risky, carried out by taking live pox virus and rubbing it into an opened wound. Recovery after inoculation took a month or more. Doctors estimated that the losses would be 2 percent. But Washington calculated that inoculation was the only way to save the Continental Army. He ordered that all those who did not have smallpox in the past must be inoculated. Newly inoculated soldiers were isolated for a few weeks so as not to spread the disease. It worked. The Continental Army was saved. Losses of inoculated troops turned out to be about 1 percent. The program was so successful in controlling smallpox that it was repeated the next winter in 1778 at Valley Forge, Pennsylvania.

Q92: Why is the first day of fall, the autumnal equinox, sometimes on September 21, sometimes on September 22, and sometimes on September 23?

. . . .

The autumnal equinox this year (2018) was September 22 at 8:54 p.m. CST. That's when the fall season began. Theoretically, the 22nd is also the day of the year when all points on the earth's surface experienced the same 12 hours of daylight and 12 hours of darkness.

A similar event takes place around March 21 and is termed the *vernal* or *spring equinox*. The word *equinox* means "equal night" in Latin.

Consider the image of the earth going around the sun in a flat plane, with the sun in the middle of that flat plane, termed the *ecliptic*. The earth spins on its axis once every 24 hours, giving us day and night. But the earth's axis of rotation is also tilted 23.5 degrees to that flat plane as it orbits the sun.

For half the year, the northern hemisphere is tilted slightly toward the sun, giving our northern hemisphere longer days, and the hotter weather of summer. The other half of the year, the northern hemisphere points away from the sun, bringing on shorter days and the colder days of winter.

It is not quite true that there are 12 hours of daylight and 12 hours of nighttime on the autumnal and vernal equinoxes. Because the earth's orbit is slightly elliptical and the light from the sun is refracted or bent as it goes through the atmosphere, we do get just a bit more than twelve hours of daylight on the autumnal equinox.

We can blame or thank Pope Gregory XIII for introducing our modern-day calendar in 1582. The Gregorian calendar was a slight modification of the Julian calendar mandated by Julius

Caesar in 46 BCE. The equinox dates change because of the difference in how the Gregorian calendar defines a year of 365 days and the time it takes the earth to orbit the sun, which is about a quarter of a day more than 365. Put another way, the earth is not in the same spot every year on a given date.

This has the effect of having the September equinox occur six hours later than the previous year's September equinox. This eventually moves the date by one day. When a leap year comes along, it sort of resets the clock.

The autumnal equinox most often happens on September 22 or 23. A September 21 equinox has not occurred since the year CE 1000. The last September 24 autumnal equinox occurred in 1931, and the next one will be 2303.

The full moon nearest the September equinox is known as the harvest moon in the northern hemisphere. The time between one moonrise and another around this period becomes shorter. Normally, the moon rises about 50 minutes later every day. Around the harvest moon, the time difference between two successive moonrises decreases to about 35 minutes for a few days. This phenomenon occurs due to the low angle that the moon's orbit around the earth makes with the horizon during this time of year.

In the old days, the early moonrise for a few days around the equinox in the northern hemisphere meant that farmers had moonlight to harvest their crops for a longer time in the evenings. In some areas of the country, the harvest moon was called the corn moon, because corn was husked by hand, very labor intensive, and farmers would go back out in the fields after milking cows to bring in an extra load of ear corn.

Q93: *How does dry ice burn your skin?*
. . . .

Dry ice is extremely cold and will actually freeze the skin. Freezing and burning feel much the same because, in both cases, the skin cells are being damaged and broken open. Touching something extremely cold makes the water in the cells freeze, forming crystals which tear through the cell membranes. You are feeling damaged cells, and it feels about the same as holding something extremely hot. Dry ice should be handled wearing gloves or using tongs.

If you briefly touch dry ice, your finger will not get wet. It feels like touching really cold Styrofoam. Holding dry ice in your hand, however, will give you severe frostbite. You definitely do not want to eat or swallow dry ice because the dry ice is so cold it can freeze your mouth, esophagus, or stomach.

If you do come in contact with dry ice for any length of time, the frostbitten skin turns white and you lose sensation. Treat the frostbite like you would treat a burn. Run cold water over the area.

Dry ice is frozen carbon dioxide and has a temperature of -110°F (-79°C). The air temperature rarely reaches even 30 below in a bad spell of winter weather.

Carbon dioxide is a natural component of air and is the same stuff we exhale. In our breathing or respiration, we take in oxygen and breathe out carbon dioxide. Dry ice is a sublimating material, which means it goes from the solid state to a gas state without being a liquid. Normal "water" ice will go through stages or states of ice (solid), then water (liquid), then vapor (gas). Dry ice skips that liquid state, moving from a solid state directly to a vapor or gas state. If you place a chunk of dry ice on a table and keep an eye on it, you notice that the chunk gets smaller and smaller, and finally disappears. No wet spot or water is left on the table.

Dry ice is made by compressing and cooling carbon dioxide (CO_2) gas until it turns into a liquid. When the pressure is suddenly released on the liquid CO_2, dry ice is created. Consumer cost is $1.00 to $3.00 per pound.

The most common use for dry ice is the storage, preservation, or shipping of frozen foods. Dry ice is used to remove asphalt floor tile. The extremely cold dry ice freezes the glue, making it ineffective, and the tiles pop right up with a slight nudge.

A CO_2 fire extinguisher works by displacing oxygen or pushing away the oxygen. The CO_2 is also very cold as it comes out of the extinguisher, so it cools the fuel as well. A CO_2 extinguisher has a hard horn, no pressure gauge, and is red in color. You find these extinguishers in labs, kitchens, storage areas, and mechanical rooms.

You may have heard of sand blasting, which is directing a stream of abrasive sand under high pressure to smooth, roughen, shape, or more often clean a surface. Less familiar is dry ice blasting. Bits of dry ice are shot, using compressed air, at a surface. It's a bit more expensive than sand blasting, but there is no waste, no toxicity, and no danger of electrical problems.

There are some fun things one can do with dry ice. A chunk of dry ice dropped in hot water will yield a beautiful and bountiful dense white fog. Tiny CO_2 bubbles are created in the water. They rise to the top of the hot water, mix with the air, and cause a sudden drop of air temperature. Cold air can't hold vapor or moisture compared to warm air. Tiny droplets of water form, producing a visible fog. The fog is a mixture of water, air, and CO_2. It is quite heavy and stays as low as possible.

The low-hugging nature of CO_2 fog has been used to purge ship holds and tanks of possible explosive or poisonous gases.

Lay a warm spoon on top of a block of dry ice and you will hear a high-pitched sighing noise. The dry ice (frozen CO_2) surface turns to gas, tries to escape, and pushes the spoon away for a short period of time. The spoon sinks again on the surface, and the process starts over, the vibration causing the sighing sound.

Q94: Do cell phones cause cancer?
· ·

This issue is quite controversial, and the jury is still out on this question. There is no clear answer. The matter garnered national attention in 1993 when a Florida man appeared on a national talk show and claimed his wife's brain tumor was caused by radio frequency radiation from her cell phone. The lawsuit was dismissed two years later due to a lack of scientific and medical evidence.

Waves used in cell phones are radio waves, which are a form of electromagnetic radiation. The energy from electromagnetic radiation sources is determined by its frequency, which is the number of vibrations per second. This electromagnetic radiation can be divided into two categories, ionizing and non-ionizing. Generally, the lower the frequency, the less energy, and the safer the radiation. Higher frequency, more energy, less safe for humans.

Ionizing radiation has enough energy to knock an electron out of orbit around the nucleus. This causes the atom to become charged or ionized. The radiation from X-rays, gamma rays, radioactive materials, radon, and cosmic rays from outer space is ionizing. Exposure to ionizing radiation increases the risk of cancer.

The radio waves used by cell phones are non-ionizing. The evidence so far indicates that the energy from a cell phone does not release enough energy to damage DNA or genetic material, which can lead to cancer. The problem is that cell phone use is relatively new. Two recent studies, one in rats and one in mice, suggest that if there is any risk, it is small. The studies were conducted over a 10-year period.

The radiation coming out of a cell phone is very much the same kind of radiation in a microwave oven, but far, far less intense. The frequencies used by cell phones are higher than FM radio, but lower than microwave oven frequencies. Does cell phone use cook the brain? Not really, because the level is so low. But long-term use? No one knows for sure. Could cell phone use affect cognitive memory function? Not sure, but the memory temporal lobes are right next to where we hold our cell phone.

There is some anecdotal support, but not scientific evidence, for a link between brain tumors and extreme cell phone use. The lawyer who defended O.J. Simpson, Johnnie Cochran, developed a brain tumor on the side of the head against which he held his cell phone. Senator Edward Kennedy of Massachusetts was diagnosed with a brain tumor in May 2008 and died in August 2009. Some believe his brain tumor was caused by heavy cell phone use. One should be careful about these kinds of stories. There has been no overall increase in the rate of brain cancers even as our use of cell phones has skyrocketed.

The amount of that radio frequency energy that a person receives varies with the distance from the cell tower, how much the cell phone is used, the length of time of the call, and the age of the cell phone. The older analog cell phones emitted more radiation than the modern digital ones.

No one knows for sure about long-term use, say over a lifetime. Most long-term studies have shown no relationship between cell phone use and cancer, or the findings have been confusing and inconsistent. Scientists do not yet know enough about frequent use, where people are on their cell phone for several hours a day. In addition, cancers take a long time to develop, particularly brain cancers.

In 2011, the World Health Organization listed mobile phone use as "possibly carcinogenic to humans." Few authoritative people claim that there is a definite cause and effect between brain cancer and cell phone use. But prudent people in the field are saying "better safe than sorry." Some recommend keeping the iPhone 0.2 to 0.5 inches (5 to 15 millimeters) from the body. Users can use speakerphones or earbuds, text instead of talk, or avoid using cell phones in buildings, elevators, or rural areas, where the cell phone has to work harder to receive and transmit signals.

Chapter Ten

Chemistry and the Atom

Q95: Is there anything harder than diamond?

Mention diamonds and most of us think engagement rings, anniversary rings, and "a girl's best friend." But diamonds are valued in industry for their use as cutting tools, abrasives, and wear-resistant protective coatings. For hardness, diamonds are the standard by which all other materials are judged.

Diamonds are formed from carbon. Carbon is one of the most common elements in the world and is one of the four essential elements for the existence of life, along with nitrogen, hydrogen, and oxygen. Humans are more than 18 percent carbon, and the air we breathe contains traces of carbon.

Diamonds are formed about 100 miles (160 kilometers) below the surface of the earth, where tremendous heat and pressure change carbon into diamonds. Most of the diamonds we see today were formed millions of years ago and brought to the surface of the earth by volcanic eruptions.

Recently, a patent was taken out for a compound of carbon and nitrogen that is said to rival diamonds in hardness. Its purpose is to serve as an inexpensive substitute for diamonds in industrial applications. This new super-hard material could be used to cut steel. Also, new man-made diamonds might be used to coat metals such as gears and bearings to make them last a lot longer.

The Mohs Scale is used to determine the hardness of solids, especially minerals. It is named after the German mineralogist Friedrich Mohs. The scale reads as follows, from softest to hardest:

1. Talc: easily scratched by the fingernail
2. Gypsum: just scratched by the fingernail
3. Calcite: scratches and is scratched by a copper coin

4. Fluorite: not scratched by a copper coin and does not scratch glass

5. Apatite: just scratches glass and is easily scratched by a knife

6. Orthoclase: easily scratches glass and is just scratched by a file

7. Quartz (amethyst, citrine, tiger's-eye, aventurine): not scratched by a file

8. Topaz: scratched only by corundum and diamond

9. Corundum (sapphires and rubies): scratched only by diamond

10. Diamond: scratched only by another diamond

Q96: What is gold used for?

Gold has the chemical symbol Au which in Latin stands for aurum, meaning "shining dawn." Gold is 19 times as dense as water and almost twice as dense as lead. A gallon of water weighs a little more than 8 pounds (3.6 kilograms), but a gallon of gold weighs 160 pounds (73 kilograms).

Despite being so heavy, gold is one of the softest and most malleable metals known. It can be hammered into a leaf or sheet so thin that it becomes translucent and light can be seen through it. An ounce of gold can be beaten into a sheet measuring 300 square feet (28 square meters). This allows gold leaf to be applied to statues or even entire buildings.

Gold is ductile and can be drawn into a very fine wire. It can be made into a thread and used for embroidery. Gold produces a deep red color used in cranberry glasses. It is such a precious metal that it has been used for centuries to "back" paper currency, the gold standard.

The most common use for gold today is in dentistry, jewelry, and electronics. Gold does not corrode easily, but it dissolves in mercury, forming amalgam alloys good for dental fillings. Nitric acid will dissolve silver and other base metals, but gold does not dissolve in nitric acid. Nitric acid has long been used to detect the presence of gold, which gives rise to the term acid test when applied to something of genuine value.

Gold by itself is too soft to be used in jewelry, so it is mixed or alloyed with other metals, such as copper, to make it stronger and tarnish-resistant. Pure gold is 24 carat gold. So 18 carat gold is 75 percent gold by weight, making 18 carat jewelry strong and tarnish-resistant. Silver is often mixed with gold to give it a whiter color.

Gold is an excellent heat and electrical conductor. It is used in wiring for special applications, such as in satellites. Gold electrical wires were also used in the Manhattan Project to build the atomic bomb, although silver was used to wrap the magnets for uranium separation. Gold is used for the more expensive audio, video and USB cables. Gold medals are given for the Nobel Prize and Olympics.

Much of the European excursion into Central America, Mexico, and Peru in the 1500s was fueled by reports of vast sums of gold. Later, in January 1848, gold was discovered at Sutter's Mill in California, and soon 300,000 Forty-Niners headed west. In August 1896, gold was found in Bonanza Creek in the Yukon, northwest Canada, and the Klondike gold rush was on.

The price of gold fluctuates on the open market. In September 2018, it was more than $1,200 per ounce.

Q97: *What causes tap water to taste more chlorinated on some days than on others?*

C hlorine is added to our water system to make water safe to drink. Chlorine kills bacteria that can build up in iron pipes. In cold weather, bacteria tend to be less active than in warm weather. At the same time, chemical reactions slow down, so the bacteria take up and process less chlorine. In the cold, chlorine also interacts less with the iron in the pipes. This can cause the water to be left with a stronger chlorine taste.

Another variable is the type of plumbing in your house. If your house has old iron pipes, you're less likely to taste chlorine because the chlorine is being used up. You are more likely to detect chlorine if you have newer PVC piping. If your house is closer to the pump site, you may notice more chlorine than if you live some distance from a well pump. If you detect a metallic taste to the water, it can be an indication that not enough chlorine is being used.

Chlorine is a halogen produced by electrolysis from sodium chloride or common salt. It reacts with most any element and is widely used as a water purifier, disinfectant, and bleaching agent. It is purchased in liquid form, at 12 to 15 percent concentration, then diluted and added at well heads or elsewhere in the system at a concentration of about 0.25 parts per million.

Chlorine has been hailed as a liberator against cholera and other water-related diseases. At the same time, overuse of chlorine has been linked to a range of human problems, including asthma, bladder cancer, and heart disease. Chlorine reacts with other naturally occurring elements to produce toxins.

A few cities, including Las Vegas, Nevada, and Santa Clara, California, treat their water supply with ozone instead of chlorine. Some people buy bottled water. Others put a container of tap water in the refrigerator. Chlorine will make its way out of the water in less than one day. There are several ways to decrease the chlorine taste in water.

Q98: What causes rubber bands to dry out and lose their elasticity?

· ·

R ubber is a polymer, made up of long chains of molecules connected together, much like long pieces of spaghetti. Any polymer that has just a few cross links between chains will be flexible. Rubber is one such polymer. Besides bending easily, rubber can be stretched to twice its original length and yet return to its original shape.

Ultraviolet light affects those chains and breaks them down, causing the rubber to dry, crack, and crumble. Any light will be a destroyer of rubber bands. The lighting in our house, either incandescent or fluorescent, contains some UV. Sunlight has far more UV.

Most everyone has experienced the dried-out rubber band phenomenon. We put a rubber band around a bunch of papers, for example, and two or three years later, the rubber band is useless. Rubber bands can last a long time if natural oil is applied, they are not stretched, and we keep them out of light. But that's not really practical. We just use a new rubber band.

Christopher Columbus and later conquistadors witnessed the native people of the Americas using a ball made from rubber trees.

Serendipity, or good fortune, led Charles Goodyear in 1839 to discover rubber as we know it. A whole bunch of inventors and scientists were trying to improve rubber. Early forms of rubber became sticky when hot, and hard and brittle when cold. Goodyear bought a patent that mixed sulfur with rubber to improve on that patent. He mixed latex rubber with both sulfur and lead oxide. The mixture accidentally fell onto a hot stove, and when it cooled, the resulting rubber was durable, flexible, and hard. His process of heating and mixing became known as vulcanization. Goodyear found that varying the amount of sulfur changed the characteristics of the rubber.

Rubber bands have some odd properties. They contract, or get shorter, when heated, unlike most solids that get longer. Stretching a rubber band causes it to give off heat. Releasing it after it has been stretched will cause it to lose heat. Try it yourself. A thick rubber band is best. Stretch it, and immediately put it to your lip. Lips are very sensitive to temperature changes. You will feel the warmth. Hold it stretched against the lips for a few seconds. Then relax the rubber band. The lip will feel the rubber band getting cooler.

Q99: How much radiation does it take to kill a person?

The short answer: A single dose of 5,000 millisieverts (mSv) will kill half the people exposed to it in 30 days. Half will live and half will die, which gives a bizarre and macabre twist to the concept of "half-life"!

The universally accepted unit of radiation today is the sievert, named after Rolf Maximilian Sievert (1896–1966), a Swedish medical physicist who made major contributions in the study of the biological effects of radiation. The older unit was the Roentgen equivalent man (REM), which is still used, along with other units that include the gray, curie, and becquerel. It can really get confusing. But remember that 1sievert (Sv) is 100 REM.

Because of the 2011 earthquake off Japan and the troubles at the Fukushima nuclear reactors, much interest and concern has been focused on radiation exposure. The millisievert (mSv) per year is the unit we see in the news. The prefix milli is one thousandth or .001.

Everything in our environment has some radioactivity—air, water, soil, rocks, trees, our bodies, simply everything. Yes, our bodies are radioactive! We all have small amounts of Potassium-40, Carbon-14, and Radium-226 in our tissue, blood, and bones. Natural background radiation varies from place to place, but typically is about 2.5 mSv per year.

Health physicists generally agree that a person's occupational exposure beyond that background radiation of 2.5 mSv should be no more than 1 mSv. Most of the radiation that you and I will be exposed to comes from dental and medical X-rays, CT scans, and flying at high altitude.

Living near a coal power plant will expose a person to more radiation than living near a nuclear power plant. Coal comes out of the ground, and stuff out of the ground is often high in radioactivity.

A dental X-ray exposes you to about .01 mSv. A full-body CAT scan is worth about 10 mSv. A gastrointestinal series X-ray will rack up about 14 mSv. The medical profession is very careful about limiting radiation exposure from diagnostic tests and even when using radiation for cancer treatment. Much progress has been made in the last 100 years.

About 1,000 mSv causes radiation sickness, which results in nausea, lack of energy, and some hair loss. Close to 100 percent of people recover. A person experiences similar symptoms when undergoing treatment for cancer. Keep in mind that 1,000 mSv is 400 times average background radiation.

Certain human activities increase your background dosage. Live in the basement? Radon gas settles in the lowest possible places. The average in US homes is 2 mSv/year, but if you live in a basement, it could be a bit higher. Smoke one pack per day? That's 9 mSv/year.

Flight crews, who spend a lot of time far up in the atmosphere, face high levels of exposure to cosmic radiation. For this reason, the CDC (Centers for Disease Control and Prevention) classifies airline crewmembers as radiation workers. The annual hit to aircrews is an estimated 3 mSv. This level beats out other high-radiation jobs, such as X-ray technicians and nuclear power workers. The flight crews on long-distance carriers are more vulnerable. Flight crews flying from New York to Tokyo need to add 9 mSv/year. The CDC has not set any official limit on the amount of radiation a crew member can receive in any given year.

Q100: *How fast does electricity move?*

There are two different ideas here. First, in computer or digital terms, we tend to think of the quantity of information that is being transmitted, not the speed. That quantity is expressed in bits, bytes, megabytes, and gigabytes. You might hear a person talk about the speed of their computer, laptop, or smartphone. They're referring to how much information is sent in a given amount of time.

The second concept is the actual speed or velocity of the electrons in wires. Electricity is the flow of electrons in a wire conductor. The amount of that flow is measured in amperes, or simply amps. The movement of the electrons is caused by a voltage or potential difference between two parts of the wire. This difference is measured in volts. In a water pipe analogy, current is like the water that is moving, and voltage is the water pressure that moves the water along.

Not to be confusing, but there are also two meanings to the speed of the electricity in a conductor. The speed of the energy, electric field, and electromagnetic wave is close to the speed of light, 186,000 miles (299,792 kilometers) per second. When a light switch is thrown on, the electric field or force is immediate in all parts of the wires and moves nearly at the speed of light.

But that is not the speed of the actual electrons in the wire. The term used for actual electron speed is drift velocity. Free electrons in a copper wire will vibrate randomly, but when the electricity is turned on, the electrons start to move proportionally to the voltage applied. That drift speed is on the order of a few inches per hour at best. In a direct current (DC) system, such as the batteries in a flashlight, the flow is "slower than molasses in January." In an alternating current system (AC), such as the wiring in a house, the electrons sit there and vibrate back and forth.

In short, the electrical energy flow is fast but the electron flow is slow. In real life, we don't care about the electron speed. We want our electricity to be instantaneous when the switch is thrown, and it is.

The typical voltage from an electric generator, powered by coal, natural gas, nuclear, or falling water, is 25,000 volts. Electrical energy is carried across country most efficiently by stepping it up to a voltage between 200,000 to 750,000 volts. Substations transform the voltage back down to the 7,200 volts for wires running around the neighborhood.

Those gray cylinder transformers on top of wooden electrical poles step voltage down to 220 volts to come into our homes. We use 110 volts for our lights, outlets, and most appliances. The 110 volts is often called 115 volts, 117 volts, or 120 volts. It's all the same. Items that use 220 volts include the electric water heater, electric stove, clothes dryer, and central air conditioning or arc welders. Most other countries in the world use 220 volts AC for everything—lights, outlets, and all household appliances.

Q101: How is natural gas different from propane that we use on our grills and campers?
· ·

Methane, ethane, propane, and butane are all gases called hydrocarbons made only from hydrogen and carbon. The difference is in how they are put together: methane (CH_4), ethane (C_2H_6), propane (C_3H_8) and butane (C_4H_{10}). For example, we can read butane as 4 carbon atoms linked to 10 hydrogen atoms. There are a few other hydrocarbons, including pentane and hexane. Hexane is the gasoline we use in our cars and trucks. A property of all hydrocarbons is that they require oxygen for combustion and that they produce heat, water vapor, and carbon dioxide when burning.

Natural gas is mostly methane (CH_4). That's one carbon atom linked to four hydrogen atoms. Natural gas comes out of the ground and is often found in the same reservoirs as crude oil and coal beds made from organic matter that decomposed eons ago. The gas must be "cleaned up" at a processing plant to remove contaminants of carbon dioxide, hydrogen sulfide, and water. Natural gas is less dense than air. If you put natural gas in a balloon, it will float upward just like a helium-filled birthday balloon.

Natural gas is the kind that travels through pipelines to cities, towns, homes, and factories for heating, cooking, etc. It has no smell, so the company adds a smelly chemical called methyl mercaptan to make it easier to detect a leak. Natural gas is sold in cubic feet, because that is a measure of gas volume.

Much of the natural gas produced in the United States is shale gas. Shale gas wells depend on fractures that allow the gas to flow easily. This hydraulic fracturing of shale formations to release the natural gas can be controversial because the full environmental effects are unknown or open to debate. One thing is clear: sand fracking has made the United States the number one gas producer in the world.

By changing the temperature and pressure, natural gas can be liquefied into what is called liquefied natural gas (LNG) for storage and transport by road tankers and rail cars to places where pipelines do not exist. Specially designed cryogenic (cooling) ships carry LNG overseas.

Propane (C_3H_8) is easy to liquefy and is stored in bottles or tanks. We can see propane tanks around houses and farms that are not served by a natural gas pipeline. Propane is also used in barbecue grills, RVs, locomotives, buses, forklifts, hot-air balloons, blow torches, as a propellant in aerosol spray cans, and in ice resurfacing machines (Zambonis).

Propane in liquid form (LPG, for liquid propane gas) can be stored in a pressurized tank, and that is why LPG is sold in gallons. The pressure keeps the propane in liquid form. When the tank's valve is opened, the LPG moves out of the tank, and when it is no longer under pressure, it turns into a gas state. Unlike natural gas, propane is heavier than air. Put propane into a balloon, and the balloon will sink to the ground.

Propane is more efficient than natural gas, yielding almost two and a half times more energy per unit volume. But propane costs about six times as much as natural gas, depending on where a person lives. This has been especially true in recent winters, as many propane users discovered. Propane is a byproduct of the oil refining process and hence the price fluctuates more than the price of natural gas.

Butane is easy to liquefy and is used in cigarette lighters and camp stoves. The propellant in some aerosol spray cans is butane. Handheld butane lighters are popular for igniting candles, fireplaces, and campfires.

Q102: *How is plastic made?*
. . . .

T he origin of the word tells us a lot. The word *plastic* comes from the Greek *plastikos*, which means "capable of being shaped or molded." That property of matter leads to seemingly unlimited versatility, as plastic objects can be plates, bottles, boxes, tubes, fibers, and films. In the last century, plastic has largely replaced traditional materials such as wood, glass, paper, stone, leather, ceramic, and metal.

Some overall positive characteristics of plastics are that they are low in cost, versatile, waterproof, and easy to make. Add that they are lightweight and durable. Objects made of plastic can be molded, extruded, cast, or blown into limitless shapes. Plastic materials can include films, foams, coatings, sealants, and glues.

There are at least 14 different categories of plastic, each with a name and letter code. They range from polyethylene terephthalate (PET) in our soda bottles to polyvinyl chloride (PVC) that goes into plumbing pipes, drain gutters, and window frames.

Most plastic stuff is made from crude oil, coal, and natural gas. The chemistry can be complex, but plastics are chains of the same molecules linked together. The chains are called polymers, most often made of carbon and hydrogen with bits of oxygen, nitrogen, sulfur, and chlorine thrown in.

Some plastics are very specialized. Polymethyl methacrylate (PMMA) is used for contact lenses and light covers on cars. Phenol formaldehyde (PF) is a heat-resistant plastic that goes by trade names of Formica and Bakelite. Polytetrafluoroethylene (PTFE) is a plastic coating known as Teflon that coats nonstick surfaces frying pans.

Extrusion is one way of molding plastics. The plastics factory in Tomah, Wisconsin, originally called Van Pak, then Union Camp, then Exopack, and now Coveris, made plastic bags for many years. Plastic pellets arrived by railcar and then were fed from a hopper into an extruder that melted the pellets. A die formed the newly made polyethylene into a ring. The ring was blown into a bubble that rose about 30 or 40 feet (9 to 12 meters). As it cooled, the bubble collapsed into a flat tube, and eventually bags were cut to size, folded, and packed. It was quite a sight to see.

The second main plastic manufacturing technique, in addition to extrusion, is injection molding. Pellets are heated and melted into a liquid state, and the plastic is injected through a nozzle into a mold cavity, where it cools and hardens to the shape of the cavity. When the plastic has solidified, the mold opens and the part is ejected.

The molds are made of aluminum or steel and precision machined to form the features of the desired part. A mold maker, or toolmaker, is a highly skilled craftsman. Injection molding is a very fast process, producing large numbers in a short time frame.

There can be a downside to plastics. The superior quality of durability means that plastics deteriorate and degrade very slowly, so landfills can quickly fill up with plastic products. We've all seen paper or cardboard boxes alongside roadways. The elements make them degenerate rather quickly. But plastic pop bottles seem to stay there forever, unless a sponsored clean-up crew picks them up.

Ever so often something comes out on the market that sounds really good, but on closer inspection, drawbacks are found. One of those is the environmentally friendly biodegradable trash bags that are said to disintegrate into compost when put in a landfill. Seems like a good idea, so what's the downside?

For one thing, biodegradable plastic bags are made from corn, potatoes, and starch, so they are not as strong as plastic bags, especially if they get wet on the bottom. A shopper could lose groceries rather quickly.

The second problem is that nothing decomposes quickly in a landfill. EPA rules demand that air, moisture, and sunlight are kept out, so few bacteria grow and nothing has a chance to biodegrade easily. When cornstarch bags do decompose, methane gas is a byproduct. Methane is a leading contributor to greenhouse gases. As an additional kick in the head, biodegradable "plastic" bags are also quite expensive. There is no easy solution.

Q103: *How was oxygen discovered?*

Many of the early discoveries in chemistry were made by alchemists. They tried to turn base metals, such as lead, into gold. The used every conceivable action, reaction, and trick to achieve this transmutation. They never succeeded, but along the way they made many discoveries.

The discovery of oxygen is attributed to Englishman Joseph Priestley in 1773. A staunch Calvinist, he prepared for the ministry, held very liberal views, and became pastor of a small congregation in Leeds. He met American Benjamin Franklin on one of Franklin's trips to London, and they became lifelong friends. It was Franklin who really got Priestley interested in science.

Priestley lived next to a brewery in Leeds. He was intrigued by the mysterious gas that floated over the fermenting liquors. He found that the gas extinguished burning chips of wood and that the mixture of this gas and smoke drifted over the side of the vat. He concluded that the gas was heavier than air. He had discovered carbon dioxide. He found that dissolved in water, it had a pleasant, tangy taste. It was carbonated water, or soda water, and for its discovery Priestley was awarded a medal by the Royal Society.

Priestley used a burning lens to focus sunlight on any chosen material sample. The very high temperatures this created caused mercury oxide to decompose and produce a colorless gas above the liquid mercury. Priestley tested this gas with the flame of a candle. He reported that the "candle produced a remarkably vigorous flame." Priestley soon discovered that his new "air" would keep a mouse alive twice as long as an equal volume of ordinary air. He also inhaled the new "air" and reported that "the feeling was such that I fancied that I felt peculiarly light and easy for some time."

The eminent French chemist Antoine Lavoisier heard of Priestley's work and carried out some further experiments. He showed that the gas was a component of ordinary air that combines with metals when they are heated. Lavoisier recognized it as a new element and suggested in 1778 the word *oxygen* (Greek for "acid former") because he thought, incorrectly, that all acids contain oxygen. He went on to show that oxygen is released and oxygen is absorbed, following the law of conservation of matter. The law destroyed the phlogiston theory of combustion, which stated that a substance called phlogiston is released when something is burned.

Priestly also reported "the most extraordinary of all my unexpected discoveries." It was his observation of a "green matter" that formed on the walls of the jars used in his experiment. He was seeing photosynthesis, the process of energy supplied by the sun, combining with carbon dioxide and water to allow organic matter to grow.

Priestley and his family suffered persecution for his religious beliefs in England, so in 1794 they all moved to America. He was already famous in America as a theologian and scientist, and the people of his new country greeted him warmly. He became good friends with Thomas Jefferson.

No such good luck for his friend and fellow scientist, Antoine Lavoisier. Not only was Lavoisier a chemist, he was also a tax collector for the ruling French aristocracy. On May 8, 1794, at age 50, his career was cut short by the guillotine. French revolutionaries branded him a traitor because he had worked for the government. His wife's father and 26 others were executed on the same day. A year and a half later, the French government found Lavoisier innocent of all charges.

Q104: What is laughing gas?

Laughing gas is nitrous oxide (N_2O); two nitrogen atoms clinging to one oxygen atom. Laughing gas is used in rocket motors, internal combustion engines, aerosol propellants, medicine, dentistry, and as a recreational drug.

For rocket motors, N_2O is employed as an oxidizer. Recall that jet engines get oxygen from air, but rocket motors must take oxygen with them. For rocket use, N_2O is stable, easy to store, safe to handle, and is nontoxic. For space travel, N_2O can be broken down to provide breathing oxygen for a crew. Robert Goddard, father of modern rocketry, took out a patent in 1914 promoting N_2O and gasoline as propellants for rocket propulsion.

Internal combustion engines (car and truck engines) use N_2O to provide more oxygen than air alone, resulting in more powerful combustion. It's no wonder then, that some race cars have N_2O injected in the intake manifold, or directly into the cylinder.

The German Luftwaffe in World War II employed N_2O to increase the power of some of their specialized high-altitude recon planes, high-speed bombers, and high-altitude interceptors. Nitro in any engine can give powerful performance. In order to use nitro, engines must be able to handle higher pressures.

Who does not like a little whipped cream on cake or strawberries? N_2O is used as an aerosol propellant in whipped cream canisters and cooking sprays. It's also used as an inert gas to displace oxygen and inhibit bacterial growth in filling packages of potato chips and other snack foods.

N_2O was used as an anesthetic as early as 1844. It was dispensed to minimize pain in childbirth, oral surgery, trauma, and heart attacks. In the early days, it was administered in a rubber cloth breathing bag. Today, N_2O is routinely used in children's dentistry or for patients with high anxiety. It is a very weak analgesic.

Starting in 1799, the British upper class held "laughing gas parties." Inhalation of nitrous oxide causes euphoria, hallucinations, and a feeling that most anything is funny. Inhaling the gas would cause the user to appear sedated or dreamy, as in a stupor. Others, in a state of euphoria, would erupt in laughter. Luckily, the effects wear off within a few minutes.

These days some people will buy those whipped cream N_2O chargers called a whippit. Whipped cream dispensers require "charger" cartridges, or capsules, that are filled with pressurized N_2O. Each cartridge is about the size of a thumb and weighs about an ounce.

The charger attaches to the dispenser, which punctures it, releasing the pressurized gas into the tightly sealed container. Gas particles want to spread out, so they naturally flow out of the opening in the cartridge and disperse into the cream in the form of tiny bubbles. When the cream is dispensed from the container, those bubbles have even more room to expand. That gives the cream a whipped, airy consistency.

There is danger lurking in the practice of huffing on a balloon of laughing gas. While you are inhaling N_2O, you are not inhaling oxygen, which is needed to keep your vital organs working. A few minutes without oxygen can have devastating consequences, such as strokes, blackouts, seizures, heart attacks, and even death.

In the past few years, 10 people in London have died from abuse of N_2O. In 2012, a famous Hollywood actress suffered a seizure triggered by inhaling N_2O. The medical profession says to just stick with breathing air, not those dangerous inhalers.

Chapter Eleven

How the World Works

Q105: What is a pencil eraser made of?

L et's face it. Everyone makes mistakes. That is why they put erasers on the ends of pencils.

The lead in a pencil is actually graphite. Graphite was used as a writing device around 1600. A ball of moist bread was used to erase unwanted pencil marks. In 1770, an English scientist, Joseph Priestley, discovered that a block of Indian rubber could "rub out" pencil marks. Hence the name rubber was born. In Great Britain, the eraser is still called a rubber.

Those first erasers were not very good. The rubber got soft in hot weather, hard in cold weather, and stinky when it degraded. In 1838, Charles Goodyear mixed sulfur with rubber and heated the mixture under pressure to give the rubber strength, stability, and elasticity. The process is called vulcanization. It's good for both tires and erasers.

The patent for sticking an eraser on the end of a pencil was granted to Philadelphian Hymen Lipman in 1858. Pencils made and sold in the United States have erasers. Most pencils in Europe do not.

Most erasers today are not made from rubber. They are made from a synthetic material, polyvinyl chloride (PVC), a durable flexible plastic. Manufacturers blend in a bit of pumice, which comes from volcanoes. The pumice gives the grit material that does the erasing. Dyes are added to give the eraser color. The most popular colors are pink, red, and green.

Eraser manufacturers started using PVCs for erasers in 1995 in response to schoolchildren's allergic reactions to latex. Yes, that PVC is the same stuff used in pipes, clothing, flooring, furniture, toys and car parts.

For pencil erasers, cylindrical ribbons of eraser material are cut into short pieces called plugs. A band of metal (ferrule) is glued onto the end of the pencil, a plunger presses the eraser plug into the ferrule, and when the glue dries, a pencil with eraser is born.

Q106: How fast does a bullet go?
. . . .

Rifle bullets vary in speeds from about 600 feet (180 meters) per second to more than 4,000 feet (1,200 meters) per second. Bullet speeds can be found on shell boxes, as well as on Internet sites such as Remington and Winchester, and in bullet reload handbooks.

A .22 short has a speed of about 1,000 feet (305 meters) per second. The 30-06 Springfield rifle, developed in 1906 with bullets that have a 0.3-inch (7.6-millimeter) diameter is popular with deer hunters. It has a muzzle velocity of about 3,000 feet (914 meters) per second. Muzzle velocity is the speed of the bullet coming out of the barrel. The bullet doesn't get any faster than that! As soon as the bullet clears the gun barrel, friction with the air slows it down. A 30-06 bullet that leaves the barrel at 3,000 feet per second has slowed to half that speed, 1,500 feet (460 meters) per second by the time it travels 1,500 feet.

Bullet speeds depend on the weight and shape of the bullet and propellant weight. The amount of gunpowder that is in the bullet also affects it speed. Another factor is the type of gun from which it is fired. Atmospheric conditions also have a slight effect. What is the fastest bullet in the world? That honor is said to belong to the Winchester .223 Super Short Magnum with a velocity of 4,000 feet (1,200 meters) per second!

By comparison, the fastest human runner does about 33 feet (10 meters) per second for short distances. A car traveling at an Interstate speed limit of 70 miles per hour is moving about 103 feet (31.4 meters) a second.

Sound travels 1,100 feet (330 meters) in a second. The SST Concorde, if it ever flies again, flies at 2,000 feet (610 meters) in a second. The Space Shuttle in orbit breezed along at 5 miles (8 kilometers) in a second. The speed is the same for the International Space Station.

Q107: What temperature is twice as hot as 0°C?

S hort answer: A temperature of 273°C is twice as hot as 0°C. Still, it's a very tricky question and one that does not lead to an easy explanation.

Part of the complexity is that we typically use two temperature scales, Fahrenheit and Celsius. Celsius is often referred to as Centigrade. The temperature can be positive or negative on either temperature scale.

Temperature has to do with how much energy there is in the air. Temperature measures average molecular motion. That energy of motion is all gone when you get down to a temperature of -273°C (-459.67°F). This temperature is called absolute zero. At absolute zero there is no movement of molecules. There is no heat.

To handle the concept of absolute zero, scientists came up with a new temperature scale called the Kelvin scale. This scale is used to calculate temperatures, pressures, and the volume of gases. The Kelvin and Celsius scales are the same, but they start at a different point. Kelvin starts at 0 degrees. Celsius starts at -273°. The conversion rule is K = C+273. On a cold winter day of 0°C (32°F), the Kelvin temperature would be 273°K. A normal body temperature is 98.6°F (37°C or 310°K). Do you feel a fever coming on?

How did we come up with 273°C as an answer to the question, "What is the temperature that is twice as hot as 0°C?" If we double 273°K (0°C), we get 546°K. That is twice as warm as 0°C. Convert that back to Celsius by subtracting 273 from the Kelvin, and we have 273°C.

While that may be a scientific answer, it does not fit our everyday sense of hot and cold. Nor does it tell us how much clothing we should wear to stay warm or how dangerous it is to work in the heat of the day. The question is sometimes referred to as a trick question or one that does not have a meaningful answer. I think it just might be a question posed by science teachers to their students to get them to think about heat, cold, temperature, calories, and multiplying by zero!

Q108: Why do people sometimes get shocks from electricity?

There are two kinds of electricity: static electricity and current electricity. First, I'll cover static electricity. The atom holds the secret of electricity. The tiny atom is made up of protons that have a positive charge, neutrons that have no charge, and electrons that possess a negative charge.

The protons and neutrons make up the nucleus, comparable to our sun in the solar system. The electrons are in orbit around the nucleus, much like the planets orbiting around the sun. Normally, atoms have the same number of protons as electrons, so we say the atom is neutral or has no net charge. Objects that have an opposite charge, like positive and negative, will attract each other.

Electrons are very mobile. When we shuffle our feet across a rug, we pick up extra electrons. We can say we are charged up!

Reach for a doorknob, and the extra electrons we carry want to jump to the metal doorknob. The bit of shock we experience is the movement of these quite mobile electrons. Static electricity shocks from rugs, car seats, or clothes fresh out of the dryer may be startling but are harmless.

The static electricity that is dangerous is lightning. That's a static discharge that can carry extremely high voltages and currents. Other harmful static discharges are those that cause explosions of gases and dust. Look up these examples: the Washburn A Mill explosion in Minnesota (1878), the *Hindenburg* airship disaster in New Jersey (1937), and the Westwego grain elevator explosion in Louisiana (1977).

The second kind of electricity is current electricity, the kind generated at a power station and distributed to all our buildings. That's the type of electricity that comes out of a wall socket and runs our appliances and lights.

If we touch a live or hot wire, our body provides a path by which the current electricity can flow. A person gets an electric shock when a current passes through the body. How dangerous and how lethal depends on several factors. If our body is perfectly grounded, such as touching a water pipe or any other metal conduit, well, that is bad news because there a clear path for the current.

The body's resistance is another factor and that resistance can vary depending on whether the skin or clothing is wet or dry. Water, perspiration, or any liquid will make the skin a better conductor of electricity.

The question is often asked: "What kills a person, the voltage or the current?" We all see these signs: Danger High Voltage. But it's really the current that does the nasty deed! Of course, the higher the voltage, the higher the current. There is really not any safe voltage level. The danger depends on the current flowing through the body, and that current depends on the voltage, condition of the body, and time of flow. As little as 20 to 30 milliamps is enough to send the heart into fibrillation, where it sits there and quivers, without the pumping that sustains life. (Recall the prefix *milli* means "one thousandth.")

The danger of electrical shocks in homes is greatly reduced by the introduction of the ground fault interrupter (GFI). Built right into the electrical outlet, the device disconnects the electricity if it detects a current leakage through any body that is grounded and touching the energized or hot part of the circuit.

Q109: Why do FM stations have such a limited broadcast range?

F M, or Frequency Modulation, is a very high frequency band running from 88 to 108 megahertz. Any high radio frequency, including television broadcast and high frequency communications systems, is made up of line-of-sight radio waves. Frequency is the number of vibrations per second. The line of sight distance depends on the terrain, the antenna height, and the power of the transmitter.

Frequency modulation means that the music or voice varies, or modulates, the main carrier wave frequency. In Amplitude Modulation, or AM, the music or voice changes the amplitude or height of the carrier wave, not the frequency.

The big advantage of FM is that the reception is crystal-clear. AM is subject to atmospheric electrical noise and static from lightning, power lines, fluorescent lights, electric motors, electric switches, and random electrical racket.

Another plus of FM is that the higher frequencies in the audio spectrum can be broadcast, which means greater fidelity, especially in classical music. AM stations are located 10 kilohertz

---

apart on the AM dial. Everything above 5,000 hertz or 5 kilohertz is cut off before broadcasting so it doesn't interfere with the next radio station on the spectrum.

FM stations are 200 kilohertz apart on the FM dial. FM stations can air any audio frequencies up to 100 kilohertz. Some audio purists say that the higher frequencies being broadcast makes FM sound better. Most people can't tell the difference. Instead, it is the clarity and absence from noise and static that draws listeners to FM. And recently the Federal Communications Commission (FCC) has allowed some widening of the bandwidth for both AM and FM.

AM signals tend to hug the earth, or go over the horizon, better than FM signals. FM signals are about 100 times higher in frequency than AM stations. AM signals bounce off the ionosphere at night. The ionosphere consists of layers of rarefied gases in the upper atmosphere caused by bombardment of the atoms by solar radiation. These layers of ions and free electrons act like giant mirrors that reflect AM signals back to Earth.

FM signals cannot be reflected back to Earth by the ionosphere. This plasma layer has a natural frequency or rate of vibration. FM signals are so high in frequency, the electrons in the ionosphere layer do not have sufficient time to generate their own electromagnetic wave to bounce back. The result is that the FM wave passes right through the electrons unimpeded and no skip occurs.

Because FM radio signals are line-of-sight, you find their transmitting antennas on the highest possible hills. AM broadcast stations need a good electrical ground, so their transmitting antennas are situated in low places, even swamps and flood plains.

A handful of FM stations went on the air in the United States in late 1930s and were used for airing the same programs as their sister AM stations. FM became popular in the 1960s because many manufacturers sold receivers that were dual AM-FM. The trend in the last few decades has AM broadcasting stations attracting talk radio, news programming, and niche programming, such as all-sports or all-country music. FM has traditionally attracted classical music and public radio. These days, those lines have blurred considerably so all kinds of programming can be found on both AM and FM stations.

There are people who prefer listening to AM. A recent post on the Internet has one fellow opining, "The atmospheric noise in a summer evening while listening to a ball game is rather soothing."

Q110: Could an earthquake sink a whole country?

Quite the opposite. Huge "megathrust" earthquakes are more likely to lift a landmass farther out of the sea. A very powerful earthquake hit the Greek island of Crete in CE 365, destroying all the towns and settlements on the island. It lifted the land 30 feet (9 meters).

The earth's crust consists of huge plates that move around and can shift huge tracts of land. This tectonic activity is what forms mountain ranges when two plates are pushed together and upward like a crease on a bed sheet.

If an earthquake occurs near a coastline, a tsunami can flood the land and make it temporarily look like the country has sunk down into the sea. After a few days, the water recedes, and sea levels remain pretty much the same.

Seismologists, people who study earthquakes, have determined there are several kinds of quakes. Some occur when one huge plate slides along another, catching on the edge and then releasing all that friction at once.

But the most destructive quakes are megathrust quakes, which occur when one plate is forced underneath another in a head-on collision. The most destructive earthquake ever recorded, in terms of human life, happened on January 23, 1556 in China. The 8.5 Richter scale quake killed 830,000 people, the number determined by tax rolls at the time.

The most destructive earthquake, in terms of human life, in North America struck San Francisco in April 1906. It measured 7.9 on the Richter scale and killed 7,000 people. Most died from fires, as gas mains broke and the buildings at the time were made of wood.

It's volcanoes, not earthquakes, that sink land. In 1883, a volcano on Krakatoa, an Indonesian island, erupted. More than two thirds of the island was destroyed. It seemed as if the island had sunk beneath the sea. In fact, rock and dirt hurled outward, and the ocean rushed in to fill the remaining crater, or caldera. Earthquakes are of less concern, scientifically, than volcanoes, which can sear and sterilize huge tracts of land around them.

The loss of life and property from earthquakes and volcanoes can be enormous. It is easy to bad-mouth both shake and bake. But people recover, and yes, they rebuild, right along earthquake fault lines and in the shadow of volcanoes that can blow up at any time.

Our planet is a dynamic engine and actually relies on quakes and volcanoes to create fertile land. Plants do very well in volcanic soils. Earthquakes bring water to arid lands. Both quakes and volcanoes slowly build mountain ranges that cause rain and snow to fall.

Q111: How does a microwave oven cook food without a burner?
. . . .

Microwave ovens are actually radar sets. Radar was developed prior to World War II in both England and the United States. Radar is credited with giving the Brits a fighting chance when German planes attacked during the Battle of Britain in 1940–1941.

The heart of a microwave oven is a vacuum tube called the magnetron. A magnetron is an electronic device about the size of your fist that creates electromagnetic waves by using electricity to heat a filament wire. The resulting electrons are caused to wiggle and emit waves of about 2450 megahertz. Microwaves are exactly like light waves, except you can't see them. The length of each wave, about 4.5 inches (11 centimeters), is too long for the eye to detect. Waves strike a fan that distributes them evenly throughout the oven. In many microwave ovens, a turntable rotates the food, so that it cooks evenly.

Most foods that need cooking or heating contain water. Water molecules are composed of bipolar hydrogen and oxygen atoms. The oxygen atom is slightly negative, and the hydrogen atoms are slightly positive. When the water molecule is struck by microwaves, it vibrates wildly and rapidly back and forth, rotating first one way and then another. This rotation happens millions of times each second. All this twisting causes friction that heats up the food. Just rub your hands together rapidly and you will notice that they feel warm. The same thing happens to the food.

Dishes contain very few water molecules so there are practically no water molecules to twist or rotate and cause friction. The only heat that the dishes get comes from the food. The dishes in a microwave do not get very hot.

The waves from a microwave oven can penetrate to a depth of about 1 inch (2.5 centimeters). The amount of microwave radiation reaching the center of a slab of meat from all sides is more than is absorbed by the outside layer. People say that microwaves cook from the inside out, which is not quite correct. What they really mean is that the microwaves are simultaneously exciting molecules all the way through the food. The cooking is done more quickly and evenly than in a conventional oven.

The center of a steak can "get done" while the outside is still pinkish. Traditional gas or electric ovens heat by conduction, and to some extent radiation, which means the outer part is cooked first and the interior is cooked last. That's what we're used to.

Several years ago, a teen in Oregon heated up a jelly-filled roll in the microwave. He wolfed it down and severely burned his esophagus. He didn't realize that the jelly interior, laden with water molecules, got much hotter than the dryer bread outer part.

Microwave ovens became popular in the early 1970s. They made a cook out of anyone who could push a button or two. Microwave ovens cook food about six times faster than conventional ovens. That is an important point for busy people on a tight schedule. Add the fact that a whole food preparation industry has arisen catering to microwave oven users.

There was a time when people were concerned about the safety of microwave ovens. "If a microwave oven can cook food, maybe it can cook me," was a common refrain. If you look closely at the glass door, you will notice a metal grid of very small holes. These holes are way too small for microwaves to get through. Also, an interlock safety feature turns off the magnetron device as soon as the door opens. Most all microwaves have two independent interlocks, in case one fails.

If you want some fun, heat a marshmallow in the microwave oven. Watch through the door as it expands and expands, and then suddenly deflates.

Q112: How can a 100,000-ton (91,000-metric ton) ship float, while a 5-ton (4.5-metric ton) truck will sink?
· ·

V ery lightweight things, like a cork or piece of Styrofoam, will float. Heavy things, like a brick, will sink. But that is not a very useful rule. The weight of an object is less important than how much water the object has to move out of the way. Whether or not something sinks or floats depends on the overall density of the object compared to water. Density is how much it weighs per volume, rather than how much it weighs overall.

The ancient Greeks were among the first to figure out how this sinking vs. floating works. They found that if you put something in a container of water, it takes up space that water previously occupied. We can name the water pushed out of the way as displaced water.

Sink or float? Compare the weight of the object with the weight of the water displaced. If the object weighs more that the weight of the water displaced, down it goes. If the object weighs less than the weight of the water displaced, it floats.

Archimedes' principle states that an object experiences an upward force (buoyant force) equal to the weight of the fluid displaced. A ship is shaped in such a way that the weight of the boat is less than the weight of the water pushed out of the way. A good portion of the interior is air. The overall density of the ship, a combination of steel and air, is less than the density of water. Because the buoyant force is greater than the force of gravity on the ship, the ship floats.

All ships up to about the middle of the 1800s were made of wood. Conventional wisdom said at the time said it was not possible to make a boat out of steel. Wood floats, steel sinks. The French and British built ironclad gunboats in the late 1850s. During the American Civil War, the Confederates' CSS *Virginia*, which was originally the USS *Merrimac*, engaged the Union USS *Monitor* in March 1862. It was the first battle between ironclad ships.

Warship sizes are generally measured in displacement. The large aircraft carriers in the US Navy fleet, such as the USS *George H. W. Bush*, the USS *Abraham Lincoln*, and the USS *Harry S. Truman* each displaces in the ballpark of 100,000 tons.

The cruise industry goes by gross register tonnage (GRT). It is found by dividing the volume of the space enclosed by a ship's hull (measured in cubic feet) by 100. With emphasis on luxury and comfort, the sizes of cruise ships have increased through the years. Some of the largest cruise ships active in the world today, such as Royal Caribbean *Oasis* class ships, weigh more than 225,000 gross tons. They can be more than 1,180 feet (360 meters) long and accommodate 5,400 guests on 18 passenger decks.

Most rocks sink, but there are exceptions. Pumice is a light and porous volcanic rock that forms when gas-rich lava solidifies rapidly. Pumice floats.

Most woods float, but there are exceptions. Some rosewoods and black ironwood are denser than water. They sink when placed in water. Ebony is a dense black hardwood that sinks. Some of these dense woods are used in making musical instruments. Lignum vitae is one densest woods known. The trees are indigenous to the Caribbean and the northern coast of South America. The belaying pins and deadeyes, used for rigging sails, aboard the USS *Constitution* (Old Ironsides) and many other sailing ships were made from lignum vitae.

The three Scheckel boys had epic sea battles on the Seneca farm in the late 1940s and into the 1950s. Our ocean was the cow tank and our ships were large hollowed-out cucumbers. The favorite battle tactic was ramming your brother's boat.

Chapter Twelve

Stuff I Always Wondered About

Q113: *Where was the first speed trap set up?*

The first speed trap was set up in 1905 when New York City Police Commissioner William McAdoo was caught going 12 miles (19 kilometers) per hour in a zone in New Hampshire where the speed limit was 8 miles (13 kilometers) per hour. Two dead tree trunks spaced 1 mile (1.6 kilometers) apart each contained a deputy inside with a stopwatch and telephone. When a speedster appeared to be going too fast, a deputy would start the stopwatch and telephone his comrade in the other dead tree trunk, along with a third deputy manning a roadblock. Commissioner McAdoo was so impressed he asked the local sheriff's department to devise similar systems for New York City.

Speed traps are entirely legal and not necessarily evil devices. Enforcing traffic laws is a normal part of police operation. Knowing that traffic laws are enforced causes people to slow down and drive prudently.

Speed limits are enforced by using a variety of devices and instruments, including Visual Average Speed Computer and Recorder (VASCAR), Radio Detection and Ranging (radar), Light Detection and Ranging (LIDAR), cameras, or sensors embedded in the roadbed.

VASCAR marries a stopwatch to a simple computer. The operator on the ground or in the air presses a button as the car passes between two landmarks that are a known distance apart. Those large white stripes along the Interstate are used by both the "bear in the air" and units on the ground. Sometimes the two landmarks are posts or signs along the highway. VASCAR makes radar detectors useless. The police aren't sending out any radar beams.

Radar sends out a series of microwaves and times how long it takes for the beam to go to the target and return. Doppler radar analyzes how the frequency of the returned signal has been altered by a car's motion. LIDAR is similar to radar except a laser light beam is used instead of a radio signal.

Radar detectors are legal throughout most of the United States. However, trying to jam police radar or LIDAR is illegal. Drivers have been known to flash their lights to warn approaching drivers of a speed trap. Some places, this practice is tolerated, while in others it is deemed illegal.

Increasingly, people tend to think that radar detectors are useless and a waste of money. That's why radar detector sales are down. Radar detectors are simple radio receivers, or light receivers. Many police do not have their radar sets on continually, but rather turn them on when they see a suspected speeder. They've registered your speed before you can even take your foot off the accelerator.

Lots of places are installing unmanned roadside radar units that flash the speed of approaching vehicles. Some are now powered by solar cells. These signs are highly effective in making people aware of their speed. They lead drivers to slow down in critical areas, such as where kids are walking to school.

There is one surefire way to avoid getting a speeding ticket: Slow down.

Q114: Why are some refrigerants illegal?
. . . .

M ost states have placed various restrictions on the use of refrigerants in the past 30 years. Wisconsin passed laws in 1990 banning the release of certain refrigerants during the service or disposal of refrigerators and air-conditioners. These refrigerants, known as chlorofluorocarbons (CFCs) and hydrochlorofluorocarbons (HCFCs) are responsible for destroying the ozone layer in our upper atmosphere. The ozone layer protects us from harmful ultraviolet (UV) radiation.

R-22, Genetron-22, and Freon-22 are code names for the most common HCFCs used in older car, window, central, and roof-top air-conditioners. The manufacture of R-22 has been banned since 2010. When service technicians repair or take older refrigerators, freezers, and chillers out of service, they put the refrigerant in cylinders and pay a company that hauls it away to be destroyed or recycled.

Modern refrigerants use fluorine instead of chlorides. It's the chlorides that damage the ozone layer high in the sky. While some older refrigeration units use R-22, all home air-conditioners take the newer R-410A refrigerant, which is environmentally friendly and more efficient. The R-410A refrigerant operates in a system with higher pressure, but can absorb and release heat faster than the older R-22. The compressors run more quietly and with less vibration. R-410A is sold under trade names, such as AZ-20, Puron, Forane 410A, and Genetron R-410A. R-410A was invented and patented by Honeywell and is the choice refrigerant for the United States, Europe, and Japan.

Companies that handle refrigerants must be licensed. The service technicians must also pass a written test to be certified. Refrigerant is not illegal in Wisconsin or the rest of the United States. Instead, improved refrigerants are used. We have agreed, as a society, to take better care of our home, a home we call planet Earth.

Q115: . Is there such a thing as centrifugal force?

There is no such thing as centrifugal force, although an object that travels in a circle *acts* as if it experiences an outward force. The amount of this force depends on the mass of the object, the speed of rotation, and the distance from the center of rotation. The greater the mass and the speed are, the greater the force. That so-called centrifugal force is often referred to as a fictitious force.

A child on a merry-go-round is not experiencing any real force outward, but the kid must exert some force to keep from flying off the ride. This centrifugal force appears real, so we use the term *centrifugal force* to explain what is happening. To stay on a circular path, the kid must exert a force toward the center, called a centripetal or center-seeking force.

Think of ball on the end of a string. The ball wants to keep going in a straight line. That is the essence of Newton's First Law of Motion, or inertia. An object in motion tends to stay in motion in a straight line unless acted on by an outside force. But it is the pull of the string on the ball that makes it go in a circle. The string provides the centripetal force. If that inward pull of the string on the ball is missing, say the string breaks, the ball will go in a tangent straight line.

You are traveling in a car with a book on the dashboard. Go around a corner or curve and notice that the book slides to the outside edge. We would tend to say that centrifugal force made that happen. But what really happened? The book went in a straight line. The car tires on the highway have enough friction to make the car go in a curve. The book on the dashboard does not have enough friction. The car is actually turning out from underneath the sliding book. From the passenger's point of view, it looks as if some mysterious force pushed the book across the dashboard.

We see centripetal forces in action all the time. During the spin cycle on a washing machine, the water in the clothes wants to go in a straight line, and it passes through the tiny holes in the barrel. But the walls of the barrel push the clothes inward. They're too big to get through the tiny holes.

Centripetal force keeps the moon in orbit around the earth. Here it is gravity providing the inward acting force. If gravity were mysteriously and suddenly lost, the moon would go flying off into space and never be seen again. It is the same idea with the earth in orbit around the sun.

Every medical lab, clinic, and hospital has a centrifuge. Typically, a blood sample in a tube is slung around at high speed. The heavier, denser material goes to the outside, which is the bottom of the tube. The lighter material stays closer to the top.

We had a cream separator on the Seneca farm I grew up on. The milk was slung around at high speed. The heavier milk slid down a series of cone-shaped disks and the lighter cream moved up the cone-shaped disks. Skim milk came out one spigot and cream came out another. The skim milk was fed to the hogs. We made butter with some of the cream and sold the rest.

You may hear in the news about different nations using centrifuges to enrich uranium. Uranium-235 is needed to make atomic weapons. But natural uranium is less than 1 percent U-235. The rest, more than 99 percent, is Uranium-238. Natural uranium is spun in a centrifuge, where the heavier U-238 goes to the outside walls and the lighter U-235 tends toward the inside, where it is collected. It takes thousands of centrifuges to enrich uranium to 3 percent for a power plant and even more centrifuges and time to get to the 90 percent U-235 that is necessary for a bomb.

Q116: Why do we have leap year?

We have a leap year every four years because the earth does not revolve around the sun in a whole number of days. There is no reason why it should. It would be a freak accident of nature if the time it took for the earth to go around the sun worked out to be exactly the same as the time for a whole number of rotations of the earth on its axis, or days.

The earth needs 365.25 days to go around the sun. That extra quarter, or one-fourth day, added up four times, means that we need to add a day to the yearly calendar every four years. That extra day, every four years, is February 29 in the Gregorian calendar that we all follow. We had leap years in 2008, 2012, and 2016, and the next ones will be in 2020 and 2024.

It gets a bit more complicated. One trip around the sun takes not exactly 365.25 days, but rather 365.2422 days. (We could say it as 365 days, 5 hours, 48 minutes, and 46 seconds.) That extra day every four years overcompensates for the error.

Here's the fix. Over a period of 400 years, the totaled errors amount to three extra days. The calendar leaves out 3 leap days every 400 years. No February 29 in the third century years, (integer or whole number multiples of 100) that are not whole number multiples of 400.

The year 1600 was a leap year. The years 1700, 1800, 1900 were not leap years. However, the year 2000 was a leap year. The years 2100, 2200, 2300 will not be leap years. The year 2400 will be a leap year. The year 2500 will not be a leap year.

Three things make a leap year. The year is evenly divisible by four. If the year can be evenly divided by 100, it is not a leap year, unless the year is also evenly divisible by 400. Then it is a leap year. If this seems complicated, and it is, just get a calendar from your closest bookstore and they are sure to have it done properly. That's what I plan to do in 2100.

The term *leap year* is derived from the fact that a fixed date on the calendar advances one day of the week from one year to the next. However, in a leap year, the day of the week will advance two days, from March forward, (no pun intended) because of the extra day of February 29.

For example, Christmas Day was Wednesday 2013, Thursday 2014, Friday 2015, Sunday 2016, Monday 2017, Tuesday 2018,

Wednesday 2019, Friday 2020. Christmas Day "leaped over" from Friday to Sunday in the leap year of 2016. Christmas Day will be "leaped over" again from Wednesday to Friday in the leap year of 2020.

It is a tradition in Britain and Ireland that women may propose marriage on leap years. In Greece, marriage in a leap year is considered unlucky. In some countries, if a man refuses a marriage proposal from a woman on leap day, he is expected to pay a penalty, such as a gown or money. In other countries, if a man turns down a marriage proposal on leap day, he is expected to buy the woman 12 pairs of gloves, supposedly to hide the embarrassment of not wearing an engagement ring.

Q117: *What is the difference between ethanol and methanol?*

Methanol, or methyl alcohol, is made from natural gas or biomass. Methanol is a simple molecule with a chemical formula of CH_3OH. Methanol acquired the nickname "wood alcohol" because large amounts of it came from distillation of forest wood. A colorless, light, volatile, and flammable liquid, methanol has been proposed as a future biofuel. The raw material would be a woody biomass. Methanol is more efficient as a fuel than ethanol, but it is poisonous to drink.

Ethanol is the alcohol that people drink. It is sometimes referred to as ethyl alcohol, pure alcohol, grain alcohol, or spirits. Ethanol is produced from plant sugars through fermentation. Its chemical notation is C_2H_6O. Ethanol can also come from petroleum, but petroleum-derived ethanol is not safe to drink because it usually contains a small percentage of methanol. That 5 to 10 percent can lead to blindness, coma, or death for the imbiber.

Ethanol is used as a solvent and is employed in flavorings, medicines, colorings, and just for burning. It is miscible, meaning that it mixes with water. Ethanol is used as an antiseptic in medical sanitizers, gels, and wipes. Because ethanol mixes with water it is an excellent solvent when added to paints, perfumes, deodorants, and markers.

Ethanol was used as a propellant by the Germans in their World War II V2 rockets. The United States, using German technology, launched Explorer 1 into Earth orbit atop an ethanol-fueled Jupiter C rocket, a member of the Redstone Rocket family. Henry Ford's Model T could run on gasoline or ethanol. Most cars on US roads today can run on 10 percent ethanol. Some vehicles can use a blend of 85 percent ethanol and 15 percent gasoline. These vehicles are known as flexible-fuel vehicles (FFV) and fuel up at the E85 pump at gas stations.

Denatured alcohol is ethanol to which additives have been mixed to discourage people from drinking it. The main additive is methanol, so you may see denatured alcohol sold as methylated alcohol. Another common additive is acetone, which is fingernail polish remover. These additives make the alcohol taste bad, smell bad, and cause a person to throw up. Some manufacturers add a warning dye to give the treated alcohol a color. Denatured alcohol can be used as a solvent and fuel for camp stoves. A jelled version is called Sterno.

Ethanol for drinking is highly taxed. But alcohol with all those additives, making it denatured alcohol, unfit to drink, is not taxed.

Larry Scheckel

Q118: *What is dew point and why does it matter?*

The dew point is the temperature to which air must be cooled for moisture (dew) to form. It is the temperature at which the water vapor in the air condenses (vapor to liquid state) and forms a liquid on some surface.

The dew-point temperature is related to relative humidity. The relative humidity is the ratio of how much moisture is in the air compared to how much moisture the air can hold. A high relative humidity means that the dew point is near the temperature of the air. A relative humidity of 100 percent denotes that the air is saturated with vapor and the dew-point temperature is equal to the air temperature. The known dew-point temperature at night is a good indication of the lowest temperature the next morning.

Heat release during a change in state is important for freeze protection of crops, such as oranges in the south and cranberries in the north country. When the air temperature gets close to freezing, the citrus farmer or cranberry grower sprays liquid water on the crop. As that water freezes, heat is released to the fruit, protecting it against the ravages of the cold. Whenever a change is made from a high-energy state (liquid) to a lower energy state (ice), energy is released to the environment.

Aircraft pilots use dew point to estimate the height of the bottom of the clouds. They also use dew point as a warning for the possibility of carburetor icing. Icing will block the flow of fuel to the engine cylinders.

As air rises in our atmosphere, it expands and cools. Cool air cannot hold as much moisture as warm air. The relative humidity automatically goes up as the air rises. At some altitude, the relative humidity has gone up to 100 percent. The dew-point temperature has been reached, and the air cannot hold any more moisture. The vapor in the air will condense on tiny particles of dust, smog, smoke, and oxygen molecules. A cloud forms.

238 Chapter Twelve

That altitude is found at the base of those fluffy white cumulus clouds. In our area, that happens at between 3,000 and 8,000 feet (910 and 2,400 meters).

What about fog? It makes sense that fog is likely to form when the dew-point temperature is within two or three degrees of the air temperature. Recall that the dew point is the temperature of the air in which dew will form. The air is saturated with moisture and cannot hold any more vapor. Vapor condenses on particles that are in the air and fog forms. Fog is really a cloud at low altitude.

There are devices that measure the dew-point temperature. A dew-point meter utilizes a polished metal mirror which has cool air passing over it. The temperature at which moisture forms on the shiny surface is read as the dew point. A person can simply watch the mirror to see when dew forms, but in actual practice, most meters use a photocell to detect when the mirror becomes cloudy.

A sling psychrometer has two glass thermometers mounted on a rectangular slab. One bulb is dry, and the other is covered with a wick, such as a piece of cloth. The wick is wetted, and the operator uses a handle to whirl the instrument around for a few minutes. The water on the wick evaporates and cools down its thermometer. Evaporation is a cooling process. The drier the air, the more the wet-bulb thermometer cools and so lower the wet-bulb temperature will go. To read the relative humidity, the user consults a table of dry bulb temperatures and the difference between the two. The sling psychrometer is the most accurate method of measuring the moisture in the air.

The hair psychrometer uses strands of human hair or horse-hair. Hair becomes longer as the relative humidity increases, shorter when the hair is dry. Levers magnify the small change in hair length. Some instruments, such as the radiosondes sent aloft daily by the Weather Bureau, use materials that vary the electrical resistance with the amount of moisture absorbed.

Larry Scheckel

Some devices, such as cell phones or sealed packages, may have a humidity indicator. They use moisture-sensitive chemicals, such as cobalt chloride or copper chloride, that change color when the humidity is high.

Q119: Why do gas gauges in cars take so long to go from full to half full, but then go from half to empty so much more quickly?

We've all experienced this phenomenon. Fill up the gas tank, start down the highway, and the gas needle sits on "full" for the first 50 to 60 miles. It seems like we're getting free mileage. Why can't fuel gauges accurately register the amount of fuel in the tank?

It has to do with how the amount of fuel is measured. Most cars and trucks use a sensor that consists of a foam or plastic float that rides up and down on top of the fuel. It's much like a fishing bobber moving up and down on water. The float is connected to a variable resistor by a thin metal rod linkage. The resistance value fluctuates as the float moves up and down.

The variable resistor is a strip of resistive material. A wiper slides along the strip, controlling the amount of current in the circuit. The gas gauge on the dashboard receives the current from the sensor, and the current goes through a resistor or a coil of wire wrapped around or sitting next to a bimetallic strip. The bimetallic strip is made of two different kinds of metals laminated together. The metals expand and contract at different rates. When the strip is heated, one metal expands more than the other. The bimetallic strip bends, with the one that expands more on the "outside." The bending action moves the needle on the gauge. That bimetallic strip is the heart of all thermostats and toasters.

When the tank is filled to capacity, the gas is higher than that float has the physical ability to rise. The float is at the top of its stroke and can't rise any higher. The float is really squished down into the gasoline. It will stay there, showing "full," until enough of that gas is used that the float is able to descend some.

It's just the opposite when the tank is near empty. The gauge will register empty even though there is still fuel in the tank. The float can no longer sink because it is sitting on the bottom of the tank. However, some gasoline is present below the float.

Automakers know all about this, of course, and they don't care. They are more concerned about people running out of gas, so they err on the side of safety. They do not want people running out of gas before the gauge reads empty. That would leave a ton of stranded, angry motorists. The gauge is designed to show empty when there is still time to get to the nearest gas station.

Most modern cars today have a microprocessor that senses the variable resistor in the tank. The microprocessor sends info to another microprocessor in the gauge on the dashboard. The microprocessor allows for a very nice feature that gives the driver some kind of warning alarm and dashboard light that comes on when there are only about 2 gallons (8 liters) of fuel left in the tank.

There are several positive features of the microprocessor. The car manufacturer can take into account the odd shapes of gas tanks. Some cars have molded tanks with weird shapes that form around various car structures.

The microprocessor can also provide some smoothing and damping of the sensor movement when the car goes up or down a hill or around a sharp turn, where the fuel is sloshing all over the place.

Q120: *Why do some chemicals explode when mixed?*

Chemical explosions are rapid and violent oxidation-reduction (redox) reactions that produce huge amounts of heat and rapidly expanding gases. A redox reaction is simply a reaction in which two atoms exchange electrons. Oxidation involves loss of electrons. Reduction means a gain in electrons. All explosions are exothermic, meaning heat is given off or liberated.

It is the speed of the reaction that makes the difference between ordinary combustion and an explosion. Consider wood that is burning in the fireplace or campfire. The same oxidation-reduction process is taking place in the burning wood as is occurring with a firecracker. However, heat and gas are released from the burning wood much more slowly, not rapidly enough to cause an explosion as in the firecracker. Another example of a very slow redox reaction would be steel that rusts.

Gunpowder was the first man-made explosive, invented by the Chinese in the ninth century CE. A combination of sulfur and charcoal was the fuel, and saltpeter (potassium nitrate) was the catalyst that provided the oxygen. Gunpowder or black powder is a slow-reacting explosion causing a subsonic (not as fast as the speed of sound) shock wave. That's good for propelling a bullet out of a gun barrel. Deflagration is the term used to describe this kind of slower burning explosion.

Nitroglycerine was discovered in 1860s. Nitroglycerine is unstable, so Alfred Nobel invented the safer-to-handle dynamite in 1866. Dynamite and TNT produce fast-acting explosions with a resultant supersonic shock wave. Detonation is the term used for a fast-acting explosion. If dynamite were to be used in a gun barrel, it would blow the gun barrel apart.

That prefix *nitro* is a clue that an explosion of some kind is possible. We burn 10 percent nitromethane fuel in our radio-controlled airplane engines. Nitromethane fuel is used in some dragster race cars. A fertilizer bomb destroyed the Federal Building in Oklahoma City in April 1995 with the loss of 168 lives. Timothy McVeigh used more than 4,800 pounds (2,177 kilograms) of ammonium nitrate fertilizer and nitromethane. There's that prefix *nitro* again.

The worst industrial accident in the United States occurred on April 16, 1947 in the port of Texas City, Texas. The French freighter SS *Grandcamp*, loaded with 7,700 tons (7,000 metric tons) of ammonium nitrate, exploded at 9:12a.m. The denotation killed 581 people and injured more than 3,500. The blast knocked out windows in Houston, 40 miles away.

An explosion of twice the magnitude of the Texas City disaster marked the N1 rocket disaster in the former Soviet Union on July 3, 1969. The Russians planned to use the N1 rocket to beat the Americans to a moon landing. A loose bolt was ingested into a fuel pump of one of the thirty engines, triggering the massive blast. After that accident, the Soviets never again mounted a serious effort to go to the moon.

Q121: *What attracts magnets to certain surfaces?*

A magnet is any material that produces a magnetic field. Most magnets are made of iron or steel. Like everything in the universe, magnets are made up of billions of atoms. Electrons orbit around the nucleus much like planets orbiting the sun. Each electron also spins or rotates on its axis.

In a magnet, the electrons spin with their axes all pointing in the same direction. The atoms in a magnet get together in small groups called domains. The axis of spin of the atoms in each domain all point in the same direction. Each has the capability of being a microscopic magnet, behaving as a tiny bar magnet. In any material that is not a magnet, the spin axis of the electrons point in random directions.

You can make your own magnet, albeit a temporary one. Take a needle and hold it against a magnet. Better yet, stroke the needle across the magnet. Many of the electrons moving around the nucleus of the atoms in the needle will begin aligning so their axes all point in the same direction. Your needle becomes a magnet on its own. Your newly created needle magnet will stick to anything steel.

Bar magnets have a north pole and south pole. Like poles repel and unlike poles attract. A north pole will repel a north pole but will attract a south pole. A horseshoe magnet is a bar magnet bent around into the shape of a horseshoe. Two poles close together can pick up more things than a single pole.

How did people come up with the names north and south pole? The north pole is that end of the bar magnet that points to the north magnetic pole when hung from a string. The north magnetic pole is up in Hudson's Bay, about 1,100 miles (1,770 kilometers) from the geographic north pole.

Many strong permanent magnets are made from an alloy of metals: aluminum, nickel, and cobalt. They are called alnico magnets, a name formed by taking the two-letter chemical symbol of each metal. These days we have even stronger magnets made from several rare-earth materials. Common ones are neodymium and samarium-cobalt.

Lodestone, or magnetite, is a mineral found in nature. It provided the world's first compasses, used by the Chinese for navigation in the CE 1100s. Extreme heat, severe jarring, or a strong alternating current field can destroy a magnet.

Magnets have many uses in addition to holding your excellent school report card on the refrigerator door. Audiotapes and videotapes have a magnetic coating. Disk drives also record information on a thin magnetic coating. Credit cards have magnetic stripes. Microphones employ magnets to convert sound to electricity. Magnets help speakers change electricity to sound. Electric guitars have magnetic pickups. Magnets are essential parts of electric motors and generators. Magnetic resonance imaging (MRI) take pictures of our insides. A compass is a bar magnet on a pivot and is free to align itself with the earth's magnetic field.

Hermann Einstein brought home a magnetic compass to his young son, Albert. The five-year old boy noticed that the needle always swung northward, seemingly guided by some invisible force. The behavior of the compass had a profound influence on him. It made him recognize there was "something behind things, something deeply hidden in nature."

Index

A

addiction 90
alopecia 38. *See* hair
altitude 10, 78, 79, 93, 111, 179, 180, 181, 203, 213, 238, 239
aluminum 61, 108, 120, 128, 154, 170, 180, 209, 244
Alzheimer's disease 18
animals 9, 45, 46, 47, 54, 58, 59, 69, 70, 73, 126, 158, 173, 174
antiperspirants 25
ants 10, 62, 63
appendix 9, 39, 40, 41. *See* digestion
Archimedes 119, 227
arthritis 20, 21
asparagus 13, 177, 178
astronauts 23, 25, 87, 111, 115, 116, 119, 179, 181
astrophysicists 93, 94
Atlantis 12, 158, 159
automobiles 156
  car accident 12, 155, 161, 162, 163
  fuel gauges 240

B

barometer 111
basalt 109
baseball 25, 26, 135, 136
  curveballs 12, 134, 135
  pitching 130, 136, 174
  player superstitions 65, 174
  sliders 12, 134
batteries 12, 141, 205
Benedictus, Édouard 155
bicycle 11, 94, 127, 128
blood 9, 18, 19, 28, 29, 30, 31, 34, 36, 48, 61, 67, 71, 80, 82, 83, 111, 126, 188, 203, 234

blood type 28, 29, 31
blue moon 11, 116, 117
Bragg, Sir William Henry 99
Bragg, William Lawrence 99, 100
brain 18, 19, 32, 33, 89, 193, 194, 195
  cerebellum 31, 32
bullets 102, 217

C

calendar 164, 189, 190, 235
  Gregorian calendar 189, 190, 235
  leap year 15, 164, 190, 234, 235, 236
cars 15, 139, 154, 156, 161, 167, 168, 206, 207, 208, 212, 237, 240, 241, 243. *See* automobiles
cats 10, 47, 64, 65, 66, 172
centrifugal force 15, 232, 233. *See* centripetal force
centripetal force 233
CFCs 231. *See* refrigerants
Challenger
  Challenger disaster 13, 179, 181
chickens 58, 59, 67, 68
Clostridium difficile 40
color
  red 198
computers 93, 170, 171, 184
cooking 10, 78, 80, 81, 160, 206, 213, 225, 226
  directions at high altitude 78
craters 11, 123, 124
crowing 66, 67

D

Daguerre, Louis 97
De Forest, Lee 171
dew point 15, 238, 239
diabetes 18, 19, 27, 41, 42, 82, 90, 91
  hyperglycemia 18

Larry Scheckel grew up on a family farm in the hill country of southwestern Wisconsin, one of nine children. He attended eight years of a one-room country school. After serving in the military and working as an engineer, he taught high school physics and aeronautics for thirty-eight years. He has won numerous teaching awards, authored many articles, and given presentations on science to thousands of adults and young people. Now retired from teaching, Larry enjoys bicycling, flying real and radio-controlled airplanes, and solving crossword puzzles. Larry and his wife, Ann, live in Tomah, Wisconsin, and love to travel.

Books by Larry Scheckel

Ask Your Science Teacher (2011)

Ask A Science Teacher (2013)

Seneca Seasons: A Farm Boy Remembers (2014)

I Always Wondered About That: 101 Questions and Answers About Science and Other Stuff (2017)

Murder in Wisconsin: The Clara Olson Case (2018)

I Wondered About That Too: 111 Questions and Answers About Science and Other Stuff (November, 2018)

I Just Keep Wondering: 121 Questions and Answers About Science and Other Stuff (2019)

Tumblehome's NSTA-CBC OSTB
(Outstanding Science Trade Books K-12) Award Winning Titles

JUVENILE FICTION
Mosquitoes Don't Bite Me (2017) 978-1-943431-30-4 (hardcover).
978-1-943431-37-3 (paperback)
The Walking Fish (2015) 978-0-9907829-3-3 (paperback),
978-0-9907829-4-0 (hardcover)
Something Stinks! (2013) 978-0-9850008-9-9

YOUNG ADULT NON-FICTION
Magnificent Minds (2015) 978-0-9897924-7-9 (hardcover),
978-1-943431-25-0 (paperback)
Remarkable Minds (2015) 978-0-9907829-0-2 (hardcover),
978-1-943431-13-7 (paperback)

Other Tumblehome Titles

NON-FICTION READS
Microplastics And Me (2019) 978-1-943431-50-2
Geometry Is As Easy As Pie (2019) 978-1-943431-52-6
Heroic Women of the Art World (2019) 978-1-943431-53-3
I Just Keep Wondering - 121 Questions And Answers About Science & Other
Stuff (2019) 978-1-943431-44-1
Inventors, Makers, Barrier Breakers (2018) 978-1-943431-42-7
I Wondered About That Too - 111 Questions And Answers About Science &
Other Stuff (2018) 978-1-943431-38-0
I Always Wondered About That - 101 Questions And Answers About Science
& Other Stuff (2017) 978-1-943431-29-8
Dinosaur Eggs & Blue Ribbons (2015) 978-0-9897924-5-5

FICTION
ResQ And The Baby Orangutan (2019) 978-1-943431-48-9
Jake And The Quake (2018) 978-1-943431-39-7 (hardcover),
978-1-943431-40-3 (paperback)
Seven Stories About The Moon (science poetry, 2018) 978-1-943431-33-5
Missing Bones (2018) 978-1-943431-34-2
TimeTilter (2018) 978-1-943431-31-1
Gasparilla's Gold (2016) 978-1-943431-19-9 (hardcover),
978-1-943431-20-5 (paperback)

Bees On The Roof (2018) 978-1-943431-24-3
Talk To Me (2016) 978-1-943431-23-6

PICTURE BOOKS
The Shooing Cave (2019) 978-1-943431-51-9
Sometimes We Do (2019) 978-1-943431-47-2
Waiting for Joey – An Antarctic Penguin Journal (2018) 978-1-943431-41-0
(hardcover), 978-1-943431-45-8 (paperback)
How the Dormacks Evolved Longer Backs (2018) 978-1-943431-27-4
Geology Is A Piece Of Cake (2017) 978-1-943431-28-1 (hardcover),
978-1-943431-46-5 (paperback)
How the Piloses Evolved Skinny Noses (2017) 978-1-943431-26-7
Stem Cells Are Everywhere (2016) 978-0-9897924-9-3
Seeking the Snow Leopard (2016) 978-1-943431-16-8
Painting In The Dark – Esref Armagan, Blind Artist (2016)
978-1-943431-15-1 (hardcover), 978-1-943431-14-4 (paperback)
Elizabeth's Constellation Quilt (2015) 978-0-9907829-1-9